Many are Called

Dag Heward-Mills

Parchment House

MANY ARE CALLED

First published by Lux Verbi. BM (Pty) Ltd. 2010

Published by Parchment House 2011
18th Printing 2018

[77]Find out more about Dag Heward-Mills at:

Healing Jesus Campaign
Write to: evangelist@daghewardmills.org
Website: www.daghewardmills.org
Facebook: Dag Heward-Mills
Twitter: @EvangelistDag

ISBN: 978-9988-8505-5-5

Dedication

To *Kate Allotey*
Thank you for doing the work of the ministry for many years as a shepherd and a lay pastor.

Contents

CHAPTER 1

Why You Are Still Alive

For we are his workmanship, created in Christ Jesus unto good works, which God hath before ordained that we should walk in them.

Ephesians 2:10

Ionce chatted with the English driver of a black cab who was taking me around central London. I asked him if he believed in God.

He said, "Certainly not. I do not believe in God."

Then I asked him, "Do you believe there is a Hell?"

"Of course not!" he retorted.

I continued, "Do you believe in Heaven?"

"I do not believe in any such thing."

Then the cab driver said to me, "Let *me* ask *you* a question."

"Of course, feel free. Ask any question you want to," I responded.

He asked me, "Do you believe in Heaven?"

"Of course I do," I answered.

"Then let me ask you another question." He asked, "If you believe you will go to Heaven, why don't you just kill yourself and go to Heaven right now. After all you would escape all the bills, debts and problems of this world."

I was shocked. I had not expected such a question. But it seemed to make sense. If Heaven was so great, what was I still doing on earth? Why didn't I just kill myself and go out of this miserable world right now.

I thought to myself, "That's a good question." But before I had a chance to answer him, we arrived at our destination.

Since that conversation with the cab driver, I have been answering his question to different congregations: Why we do not go to Heaven immediately after we are saved!

Even though God has touched our lives and given us the promise of Heaven, there is work to be done on earth. There are things to accomplish for God. God expects us to respond to His great love by giving ourselves to His work.

When we come to Jesus, He takes away our burden of sin and darkness and gives us His burden. "Come unto me, all ye that labour and are heavy laden, and I will give you rest. TAKE MY

YOKE UPON YOU, and learn of me; for I am meek and lowly in heart: and ye shall find rest unto your souls" (Matthew 11:28-29). What is the burden of Christ? It is the burden of the lost souls of this world.

It is amazing that most Christians live out their lives without realizing that the reason for their being alive is so that they can do something for God. They are not alive so that they can build houses and acquire the good things of this world. They are not alive so that they can acquire more money and lay up treasures in this world. We have only one reason to be alive, and that is to serve the Saviour who gave up everything for us. It is a sad reality that much of the teaching in the body of Christ leads Christians away from their true purpose for being alive.

"Let's think about our God, our Saviour and our King. The One who gave it all. He gave up everything...So we could be His friends."[1] I know that we rarely think about our Saviour and our King. We rarely think about the One who gave it all. That is why we rarely give up everything. That is why we are so barren and so fruitless in the kingdom.

.[1] Lyrics from Tommy Walker's, *Let's Think about Our God.*

CHAPTER 2

Many Christians Are Called

If you were God and you had six billion people to save, what would you do? Would you send one or two people to save them or would you send a lot of people? Of course, you would send many people into the fields of harvest. And that is exactly what God has done. *He has called many people!* Do not be deceived by the few pastors you see sitting on the front rows of churches. That always gives the impression that a few have been called, or that the majority of the congregation have *not* been called. Actually, it is the exact opposite. *Many,* and not just a few pastors, are called to the work of saving the world.

Five Facts about the Call of God

1. **Many are called.**

   For many are called, but few are chosen.
                                                    Matthew 22:14

What Does "Many are Called" Mean?

Many are called means *large numbers* of people are called.

Many are called means *the masses* are called.

Many are called means *huge numbers* of people are called.

Many are called means *numerous* people are called.

Many are called means *countless* people are called.

Many are called means *lots of people* have been called.

Many are called means *the majority* of the people are called.

Many are called means *most* of the people are called.

Sadly, most pastors treat their congregations as people who do not have a call. They relate to them as people who cannot do much for God. Most pastors teach their congregations how to have "a better life". Much of the preaching is about ourselves, our lives, our marriages, our homes, our finances, etc. This kind of preaching is what creates the large, selfish and barren congregations of today.

Pastors, apostles, evangelists, and teachers are supposed to perfect the saints *so that the saints do the work* of the ministry. Even the evangelist who is typically expected to be harvesting souls has a primary job of perfecting the saints for the work of the ministry. "And he gave some, apostles; and some, prophets; and some, evangelists; and some, pastors and teachers; for the perfecting of the saints, for the work of the ministry, for the edifying of the body of Christ" (Ephesians 4:11-12).

2. There is a call to fruitfulness.

"You don't need to hear a call; you're already called."

Keith Green

What are we called to do? Are we all called to be apostles, prophets, evangelists and teachers? The answer is a simple, "No." Most of us do not have these fantastic high callings. *We are all simply called to be fruitful.*

> **Ye have not chosen me, but I have chosen you, and ordained you, that ye should go and bring forth fruit, and that your fruit should remain: that whatsoever ye shall ask of the Father in my name, he may give it you.**
>
> **John 15:16**

If we were to follow our Christian teachings to their logical conclusions, most Christians would become sacrificial and do something for God. The saddest, and perhaps, ugliest feature of many Christians today is how little we do for Christ. We have been saved by an amazing act of love and grace, but we are not prepared to give up anything to save others. It is so sad to see Christians waste their lives away, doing nothing for the Lord.

3. **Some people are called in a spectacular way.**

> **And as he journeyed, he came near Damascus: and suddenly there shined round about him a light from heaven: and he fell to the earth, and heard a voice saying unto him, Saul, Saul, why persecutest thou me? And he said, Who art thou, Lord? And the Lord said, I am Jesus whom thou persecutest: it is hard for thee to kick against the pricks. And he trembling and astonished said, Lord, what wilt thou have me to do? And the Lord said unto him, Arise, and go into the city, and it shall be told thee what thou must do.**
>
> **Acts 9:3-6**

The apostle Paul was called in a dramatic and spectacular fashion. He saw a shining light come down from Heaven and heard a voice speaking to him. He fell to the ground and was struck with blindness for several days. Unfortunately, whenever someone shares an experience he had, everyone wants to have the same experience. Everybody wants to see a light and hear a voice; otherwise, they will not believe they are called. But God cannot be put into a box and He cannot be expected to repeat Himself in the same predictable way time and time again.

I remember reading about how Kenneth Hagin was healed from a heart disease and how he rose up from a deathbed. One day, I was ill and I tried to simulate the same experience. I tell you, my dear friend, I almost lost my life trying to experience the same thing that Kenneth Hagin had experienced. Believe me, God has different ways of dealing with different people.

4. Some people are called in an ordinary way.

"And he said, Go forth, and stand upon the mount before the LORD. And, behold, the LORD passed by, and a great and strong wind rent the mountains, and brake in pieces the rocks before the LORD; but the LORD was not in the wind: and after the wind an earthquake; but the LORD was not in the earthquake: and after the earthquake a fire; but the LORD was not in the fire: and after the fire a still small voice" (1 Kings 19:11-12).

It is great to experience God in some dramatic fashion. We all long for spectacular experiences with God. As a preacher, I have longed for spectacular experiences so that I could come and tell the congregation about what I had experienced. I always felt it would make me look more powerful. Mercy!

In my estimation, most people are called in an ordinary way and this makes them ignore their calling. As I preach about people being called, I realize how it awakens something that is deep within them. Many people are called but they simply do not know it. They are looking for the call in a spectacular way. But the call often comes in an ordinary way. Senior prophets like Elijah made the mistake of looking for God's call in a dramatic and spectacular way. If you continue to look for the call of God in that way, you will miss your blessing. "...And, behold, the Lord passed by, and a great and strong wind rent the mountains, and brake in pieces the rocks before the Lord; but the Lord was not in the wind: and after the wind an earthquake; but the Lord was not in the earthquake: And after the earthquake a fire; but the Lord was not in the fire: and after the fire A STILL SMALL VOICE. And it was so, when Elijah heard it, that he wrapped his face in his mantle, and went out, and stood in the entering in of the cave. AND, BEHOLD, THERE CAME A VOICE UNTO HIM, and said, What doest thou here, Elijah? (1 Kings 19:11-13).

5.   Some people are called through their desires.

**This is a true saying, if a man desire the office of a
bishop, he desireth a good work.**

1 Timothy 3:1

This is the way I received my calling. I did not have all the
dramatic experiences that people speak about. I am constantly
amazed when I hear of how people receive their call to the
ministry. I have had no such dramatic encounters but I believe
I am genuinely called by God. I did not see a light or hear any
voices. Jesus has never appeared to me commissioning me to
go into the world of ministry. Yet I believe that I am genuinely
commissioned for ministry.

I remember once when a brother came to stay in my home for
a weekend. Some months later he told me about an encounter
that he had had with the Lord in my house. He was my guest and
he was staying upstairs with the rest of the family. He described
how one night, the door opened suddenly and the Lord Jesus
entered the room. He told me how the Lord Jesus put something
in his hand and told him that He had commissioned him for a
great work.

I could not believe what I was hearing – Jesus appearing to
a visitor in my house! As this brother continued to describe his
encounter with the Lord, I became more and more angry but I
could not show my anger. I had to pretend that I was happy about
his encounter with Jesus.

"This is what I have been praying for," I thought to myself. I
was angry with the Lord because I reasoned, "Why should Jesus
come to my house, bypass (me) the owner, host and landlord and
visit someone who was just spending a night as a guest."

"How unfair could the Lord be," I thought.

I had prayed for years and years that Jesus would appear to
me. I desperately wanted to be like Kenneth Hagin who could
describe personal visits of Jesus and the hours of discussions he
had had with the Lord on various matters concerning the ministry.

How come this was not happening to me? Why was it happening to visitors in my house?

However, in spite of the absence of such visions, the Lord has given me a ministry. Because I have not had such spectacular encounters, I can encourage others who have also not had such visions to believe in God and to believe in their callings.

CHAPTER 3

How Different People Were Called

God has many ways by which He calls His servants. Unfortunately, you cannot program God into a particular mode. He simply does not fit into any of the patterns that we would like Him to fall into.

God is not a computer who can be programmed to behave in the same way every time. Every time you press Control 'S' the computer saves something. Every time you press Control 'C' the computer copies something. Every time you press Control 'V' the computer pastes what has been copied. The computer never varies its response to the same command. That is a computer, but that is not God!

God will not call people in the same way every time. The way He spoke to me may be completely different from the way He will speak to you. For instance, Paul urged Timothy to look for people who have a desire to work for Him. But in the life of Moses, we see how someone who *did not* have any desire for a divine appointment was called. I want to share with you several different methods by which God may call you to work for Him.

1. The divine call of Paul through quiet convictions:

> For though I preach the gospel, I have nothing to glory of: for NECESSITY IS LAID UPON ME; yea, woe is unto me, if I preach not the gospel!
>
> 1 Corinthians 9:16

There is nothing as important as a personal conviction to serve the Lord. Many times I have felt the dread of not following the Lord in the ministry. I am deeply convicted that I must be in the ministry and do nothing else for the rest of my life. Without such a conviction, you may not survive the different experiences, trials and battles that await those committed to the Lord.

2. The divine call of Abraham through the Word of the Lord:

> Now THE LORD HAD SAID UNTO ABRAM, Get thee out of thy country, and from thy kindred, and from thy father's house, unto a land that I will shew thee: and I will make of thee a great nation, and I will bless thee, and make thy name great; and thou shalt be a blessing: and I will bless them that bless thee, and curse him that curseth thee: and in thee shall all families of the earth be blessed. So Abram departed, as the LORD had spoken unto him; and Lot went with him: and Abram was seventy and five years old when he departed out of Haran.
>
> Genesis 12:1-4

3. The divine call of Jacob through a dream:

> And Jacob went out from Beer-sheba, and went toward Haran. And he lighted upon a certain place, and tarried there all night, because the sun was set; and he took of the stones of that place, and put them for his pillows, and lay down in that place to sleep.
>
> AND HE DREAMED, AND BEHOLD A LADDER set up on the earth, and the top of it reached to heaven: and behold the angels of God ascending and descending on it.

And, behold, the LORD stood above it, and said, I am the LORD God of Abraham thy father, and the God of Isaac: the land whereon thou liest, to thee will I give it, and to thy seed; and thy seed shall be as the dust of the earth, and thou shalt spread abroad to the west, and to the east, and to the north, and to the south: and in thee and in thy seed shall all the families of the earth be blessed.

And, behold, I am with thee, and will keep thee in all places whither thou goest, and will bring thee again into this land; for I will not leave thee, until I have done that which I have spoken to thee of. And Jacob awaked out of his sleep, and he said, Surely the LORD is in this place; and I knew it not.

Genesis 28:12-16

4. The divine call of Moses through an unusual and unnatural occurrence that drew his attention:

Now Moses kept the flock of Jethro his father in law, the priest of Midian: and he led the flock to the backside of the desert, and came to the mountain of God, even to Horeb. And THE ANGEL OF THE LORD APPEARED UNTO HIM IN A FLAME OF FIRE out of the midst of a bush: and he looked, and, behold, the bush burned with fire, and the bush was not consumed.

And Moses said, I will now turn aside, and see this great sight, why the bush is not burnt. And when the LORD saw that he turned aside to see, God called unto him out of the midst of the bush, and said, Moses, Moses. And he said, Here am I.

Ad he said, Draw not nigh hither: put off thy shoes from off thy feet, for the place whereon thou standest is holy ground. Moreover he said, I am the God of thy father, the God of Abraham, the God of Isaac, and the God of Jacob. And Moses hid his face; for he was afraid to look upon God.

Exodus 3:1-6

5. **The divine call of Aaron through Moses:**

And the anger of the LORD was kindled against Moses, and he said, is not Aaron the Levite thy brother? I know that he can speak well. And also, behold, he cometh forth to meet thee: and when he seeth thee, he will be glad in his heart.

And THOU SHALT SPEAK UNTO HIM, AND PUT WORDS IN HIS MOUTH: and I will be with thy mouth, and with his mouth, and will teach you what ye shall do.

And he shall be thy spokesman unto the people: and he shall be, even he shall be to thee instead of a mouth, and thou shalt be to him instead of God.

Exodus 4:14-16

6. **The divine call of Joseph through his childhood dreams:**

And JOSEPH DREAMED A DREAM, and he told it his brethren: and they hated him yet the more. And he said unto them, Hear, I pray you, this dream which I have dreamed:

For, behold, we were binding sheaves in the field, and, lo, my sheaf arose, and also stood upright; and, behold, your sheaves stood round about, and made obeisance to my sheaf. And his brethren said to him, Shalt thou indeed reign over us? Or shalt thou indeed have dominion over us? And they hated him yet the more for his dreams, and for his words.

AND HE DREAMED YET ANOTHER DREAM, and told it his brethren, and said, Behold, I have dreamed a dream more; and, behold, the sun and the moon and the eleven stars made obeisance to me. And he told it to his father, and to his brethren: and his father rebuked him, and said unto him, what is this dream that thou hast dreamed? Shall I and thy mother and thy brethren indeed come to bow down ourselves to thee to the earth?

Genesis 37:5-10

7. **The divine call of Joshua when Moses sent him:**

And MOSES SAID UNTO JOSHUA, CHOOSE US OUT MEN, and go out, fight with Amalek: to morrow I will stand on the top of the hill with the rod of God in mine hand. So Joshua did as Moses had said to him, and fought with Amalek: and Moses, Aaron, and Hur went up to the top of the hill. And it came to pass, when Moses held up his hand, that Israel prevailed: and when he let down his hand, Amalek prevailed.

Exodus 17:9-11

8. **The divine call of Samuel by staying in the church and being trained to recognize God's voice, which sounds like a man's voice:**

And the child Samuel ministered unto the LORD before Eli. And the word of the LORD was precious in those days; there was no open vision.

And it came to pass at that time, when Eli was laid down in his place, and his eyes began to wax dim, that he could not see; and ere the lamp of God went out in the temple of the LORD, where the ark of God was, and Samuel was laid down to sleep; THAT THE LORD CALLED SAMUEL: and he answered, here am I.

And he ran unto Eli, and said, Here am I; for thou calledst me. And he said, I called not; lie down again. And he went and lay down.

AND THE LORD CALLED YET AGAIN, Samuel. And Samuel arose and went to Eli, and said, Here am I; for thou didst call me. And he answered, I called not, my son; lie down again. Now Samuel did not yet know the LORD, neither was the word of the LORD yet revealed unto him.

AND THE LORD CALLED SAMUEL AGAIN THE THIRD TIME. And he arose and went to Eli, and said, Here am I; for thou didst call me. And Eli perceived that the LORD had called the child.

Therefore Eli said unto Samuel, Go, lie down: and it shall be, if he call thee, that thou shalt say, Speak, LORD; for thy servant heareth. So Samuel went and lay down in his place. And the LORD came, and stood, and called as at other times, Samuel, Samuel. Then Samuel answered, Speak; for thy servant heareth.

1 Samuel 3:1-10

9.   The divine call of Elisha by having a mantle thrown on him:

So he departed thence, and found Elisha the son of Shaphat, who was plowing with twelve yoke of oxen before him, and he with the twelfth: and ELIJAH PASSED BY HIM, AND CAST HIS MANTLE UPON HIM.

1Kings 19:19

10.   The divine call of Jeroboam through the word of the prophet:

And it came to pass at that time when Jeroboam went out of Jerusalem, that the prophet Ahijah the Shilonite found him in the way; and he had clad himself with a new garment; and they two were alone in the field: And Ahijah caught the new garment that was on him, and rent it in twelve pieces:

AND HE SAID TO JEROBOAM, Take thee ten pieces: for thus saith the LORD, the God of Israel, Behold, I will rend the kingdom out of the hand of Solomon, and will give ten tribes to thee: (But he shall have one tribe for my servant David's sake, and for Jerusalem's sake, the city which I have chosen out of all the tribes of Israel:) Because that they have forsaken me, and have worshipped Ashtoreth the goddess of the Zidonians, Chemosh the god of the Moabites, and Milcom the god of the children of Ammon, and have not walked in my ways, to do that which is right in mine eyes, and to keep my statutes and my judgments, as did David his father.

Howbeit I will not take the whole kingdom out of his hand: but I will make him prince all the days of his life for David my servant's sake, whom I chose, because he kept my commandments and my statutes:

But I will take the kingdom out of his son's hand, and will give it unto thee, even ten tribes.

And unto his son will I give one tribe, that David my servant may have a light alway before me in Jerusalem, the city which I have chosen me to put my name there.

And I will take thee, and thou shalt reign according to all that thy soul desireth, and shalt be king over Israel.

And it shall be, if thou wilt hearken unto all that I command thee, and wilt walk in my ways, and do that is right in my sight, to keep my statutes and my commandments, as David my servant did; that I will be with thee, and build thee a sure house, as I built for David, and will give Israel unto thee.

1 Kings 11:29-38

11. The divine call of David through the anointing of the prophet:

And Samuel said unto Jesse, Are here all thy children? And he said, There remaineth yet the youngest, and, behold, he keepeth the sheep. And Samuel said unto Jesse, Send and fetch him: for we will not sit down till he come hither.

And he sent, and brought him in. Now he was ruddy, and withal of a beautiful countenance, and goodly to look to. And the LORD said, Arise, anoint him: for this is he.

Then SAMUEL TOOK THE HORN OF OIL, AND ANOINTED HIM in the midst of his brethren: and the Spirit of the LORD came upon David from that day forward. So Samuel rose up, and went to Ramah.

1 Samuel 16:11-13

12. The divine call of Solomon through a double dream:

And the LORD was angry with Solomon, because his heart was turned from THE LORD GOD OF ISRAEL, WHICH HAD APPEARED UNTO HIM TWICE, And had commanded him concerning this thing, that he should not go after other gods: but he kept not that which the LORD commanded. Wherefore the LORD said unto Solomon, Forasmuch as this is done of thee, and thou hast not kept my covenant and my statutes, which I have commanded thee, I will surely rend the kingdom from thee, and will give it to thy servant. Notwithstanding in thy days I will not do it for David thy father's sake: but I will rend it out of the hand of thy son.

1 Kings 11:9-12

13. The divine call of Isaiah through a vision:

In the year that king Uzziah died I SAW ALSO THE LORD sitting upon a throne, high and lifted up, and his train filled the temple. Also I heard the voice of the Lord, saying, whom shall I send, and who will go for us?

Then said I, Here am I; send me. And he said, Go, and tell this people…

Isaiah 6:1, 8-9

14. The divine call of Ezekiel through the Word of the Lord:

In the fifth day of the month, which was the fifth year of king Jehoiachin's captivity, THE WORD OF THE LORD CAME EXPRESSLY UNTO EZEKIEL THE PRIEST, the son of Buzi, in the land of the Chaldeans by the river Chebar; and the hand of the LORD was there upon him.

Ezekiel 1:2-3

15. The divine call of Jeremiah through the Word of the Lord:

The words of Jeremiah the son of Hilkiah, of the priests that were in Anathoth in the land of Benjamin: To whom the word of the LORD came in the days of Josiah the son of Amon king of Judah, in the thirteenth year of his reign.

It came also in the days of Jehoiakim the son of Josiah king of Judah, unto the end of the eleventh year of Zedekiah the son of Josiah king of Judah, unto the carrying away of Jerusalem captive in the fifth month.

Then THE WORD OF THE LORD CAME UNTO ME, saying, before I formed thee in the belly I knew thee; and before thou camest forth out of the womb I sanctified thee, and I ordained thee a prophet unto the nations. Then said I, Ah, Lord GOD! behold, I cannot speak: for I am a child.

But the LORD said unto me, Say not, I am a child: for thou shalt go to all that I shall send thee, and whatsoever I command thee thou shalt speak. Be not afraid of their faces: for I am with thee to deliver thee, saith the LORD. Then the LORD put forth his hand, and touched my mouth.

And the LORD said unto me, Behold, I have put my words in thy mouth. See, I have this day set thee over the nations and over the kingdoms, to root out, and to pull down, and to destroy, and to throw down, to build, and to plant.

Jeremiah 1:1-10

16. The divine call of Peter, Andrew, James and John by being asked to follow:

And Jesus, walking by the sea of Galilee, saw two brethren, Simon called Peter, and Andrew his brother, casting a net into the sea: for they were fishers. AND HE SAITH UNTO THEM, FOLLOW ME, and I will make you fishers of men. And they straightway left their nets, and followed him. And going on from thence, he saw other two brethren, James the son of Zebedee, and John his brother, in a ship with Zebedee their father, mending their nets; and he called them. And they immediately left the ship and their father, and followed him.

Matthew 4:18-22

17. The divine call of Paul through spectacular and supernatural visitations:

And Saul, yet breathing out threatenings and slaughter against the disciples of the Lord, went unto the high priest, and desired of him letters to Damascus to the synagogues, that if he found any of this way, whether they were men or women, he might bring them bound unto Jerusalem. And as he journeyed, he came near Damascus: AND SUDDENLY THERE SHINED ROUND ABOUT HIM A LIGHT FROM HEAVEN: And he fell to the earth, and heard a voice saying unto him, Saul, Saul, why persecutest thou me?

And he said, Who art thou, Lord? And the Lord said, I am Jesus whom thou persecutest: it is hard for thee to kick against the pricks.

And he trembling and astonished said, Lord, what wilt thou have me to do? And the Lord said unto him, Arise, and go into the city, and it shall be told thee what thou must do.

And the men which journeyed with him stood speechless, hearing a voice, but seeing no man. And Saul arose from the earth; and when his eyes were opened, he saw no man: but they led him by the hand, and brought him into Damascus. And he was three days without sight, and neither did eat nor drink.

Acts 9:1-9

18. The divine call of Timothy through his family upbringing and the hand of Paul:

When I call to remembrance THE UNFEIGNED FAITH that is in thee, WHICH DWELT FIRST IN THY GRANDMOTHER LOIS, and THY MOTHER EUNICE;

and I am persuaded that IN THEE ALSO. Wherefore I put thee in remembrance that thou stir up the gift of God, which is in thee by the putting on of my hands.

2 Timothy 1:5-6

This charge I commit unto thee, son Timothy, according to the prophecies which went before on thee, that thou by them mightest war a good warfare;

1 Timothy 1:18

Thou therefore, my son, be strong in the grace that is in Christ Jesus.

2 Timothy 2:1

Who hath saved us, and called us with an holy calling, not according to our works, but according to his own purpose and grace, which was given us in Christ Jesus before the world began,

2 Timothy 1:9

CHAPTER 4

Characteristics of "Called" People

1.   God calls *FAILURES*.

> And Moses said unto God, Who am I, that I should go unto Pharaoh, and that I should bring forth the children of Israel out of Egypt?
>
> Exodus 3:11

Moses failed to deliver the people in the first instance, but God chose him even though he had failed to deliver the people. Are you a failure in any way? Many people have failed in their life's assignment but God still "calls" failures.

2.   God calls *UNWORTHY PEOPLE*.

> And Moses said unto God, *Who am I,* that I should go unto Pharaoh, and that I should bring forth the children of Israel out of Egypt?
>
> Exodus 3:11

If you examine yourself honestly, you will realise how unworthy you are. But it will be your ability to overcome this sense of unworthiness that will release you into ministry. Do not let the feelings of unworthiness keep you from obeying your call. We all know we are unworthy.

If you hold back from obeying God because of your unworthiness, you would have become the biggest fool on earth. God "calls" unworthy people and He is calling you.

3. God calls people who have been *REJECTED*.

And he looked this way and that way, and when he saw that there was no man, he slew the Egyptian, and hid him in the sand.

And when he went out the second day, behold, two men of the Hebrews strove together: and he said to him that did the wrong, Wherefore smitest thou thy fellow?

And he said, *Who made thee a prince and a judge over us?* intendest thou to kill me, as thou killedst the Egyptian? And Moses feared, and said, Surely this thing is known.

Exodus 2:12-14

Rejection is part of this life. Rejection is a very painful experience. To be rejected is to feel disliked, disrespected and unwanted. I have been rejected many times. There are many times that I have felt disrespected, disliked and unwanted. It is not easy to go through rejection. And yet, most people will experience rejection as part of their spiritual journey.

Someone said, "Before you are fully accepted, you must be rejected!"

The patterns in the Bible do reveal that most people were first rejected before they were fully accepted. Jesus Christ was rejected by the Jews before He was accepted as the Saviour. Moses was similarly rejected by his people, but was later accepted as the deliverer of Israel from the hands of the Egyptians.

4. God calls people who are *NOT BELIEVABLE*.

And Moses answered and said, *But, behold, they will not believe me*, nor hearken unto my voice: for they will say, The LORD hath not appeared unto thee.

Exodus 4:1

It is true that there is nothing about you that would particularly make people believe in God. Most of us are just ordinary people with nothing special about us. In spite of this, God uses ordinary people like you and me. It is amazing that He gets His work done with people who are not readily credible or believable. Dear friend, have faith in God. If He can raise up stones to worship Him, then He can use you.

5. God calls people with an *INFERIORITY COMPLEX*.

> Then Moses said to the LORD, "Please, Lord, I have never been eloquent, neither recently nor in time past, nor since You have spoken to Your servant; for I am slow of speech and slow of tongue."
>
> Exodus 4:10 (NASB)

All of us have things about us that give us an inferiority complex! Your inferiority complex makes you feel that God should choose somebody else. Moses felt that he could not speak as well as other people, so he asked the Lord to send someone else. Be careful with your prayer requests because God got angry with Moses for constantly questioning his call. God had invested in him over the years. God had protected him from the Egyptians and trained him in the Egyptian palaces. When it was time for him to step out in ministry he gave excuses. But there is no excuse, no matter how humble-sounding it is, that is good enough for you to reject the call of God.

6. God calls people who have *FAILED AT EARLIER ATTEMPTS* in ministry.

> And Moses returned unto the LORD, and said, Lord, wherefore hast thou so evil entreated this people? why is it that thou hast sent me? For since I came to Pharaoh to speak in thy name, he hath done evil to this people; neither hast thou delivered thy people at all.
>
> Exodus 5:22-23

The miracles of Moses did not have the effect Moses expected. Moses was disappointed in God and in himself. Perhaps you have had some disastrous disappointments in the ministry. These disappointments should not be taken as indications of whether you are called or not. Being called has nothing to do with things working or things not working out! Being called is all about your conviction of God having appointed you to His service.

> And afterward Moses and Aaron went in, and told Pharaoh, Thus saith the LORD God of Israel, Let my people go, that they may hold a feast unto me in the wilderness. And Pharaoh said, Who is the LORD, that I should obey his voice to let Israel go? I know not the LORD, neither will I let Israel go.
>
> And they said, The God of the Hebrews hath met with us: let us go, we pray thee, three days' journey into the desert, and sacrifice unto the LORD our God; lest he fall upon us with pestilence, or with the sword. And the king of Egypt said unto them, wherefore do ye, Moses and Aaron, let the people from their works? Get you unto your burdens.
>
> And Pharaoh said, Behold, the people of the land now are many, and ye make them rest from their burdens. And Pharaoh commanded the same day the taskmasters of the people, and their officers, saying, ye shall no more give the people straw to make brick, as heretofore: let them go and gather straw for themselves.
>
> Exodus 5:1-7

7. God calls people who are *NOT ELOQUENT.*

> Then said I, Ah, Lord GOD! *Behold, I cannot speak:* for I am a child.
>
> Jeremiah 1:6

An eloquent person expresses himself readily, clearly and effectively. The prophet Jeremiah knew that he could not express himself very well and he said so. This is a common complex that people who are "called" have. When you listen to eloquent preachers who have been in ministry for years, you wonder if you will ever be able to speak like them. With such shining examples before you it is always easier to remain in your world of anonymity. When God called me to the ministry, my greatest problem was my inability to speak in public.

I sought out the leader of our fellowship and asked him to pray for me because my greatest problem was my inability to stand before a group of people and speak. I remember when I knelt down to be prayed for about this problem.

Today, I am able to preach to many people in spite of this initial difficulty. Do not be worried if you are not a good speaker. God does call people who are not good speakers and turns them into preachers *par excellence*.

8. God calls *YOUNG* people.

Then said I, Ah, Lord GOD! behold, I cannot speak: *for I am a child*.

Jeremiah 1:6

Many young people reject the call because they feel that they are too young for something as noble and distinguished as the ministry. Another reason why young people stay away from ministry is because of their sexual proclivity and numerous temptations. The sexual feeling is so base in its nature that it is followed by feelings of unworthiness and carnality.

Many young people wish they were without those feelings so they could serve the Lord in holiness. God called me as a young person and I constantly battled with these feelings of unworthiness. Because of this, I was very happy to discover that Elijah was a man of *like passions*. Did Elijah really have the same passions, as I seemed to be having? This encouraged me to carry on in the ministry even though I was a very young boy.

When I discovered that Levites were to serve the Lord from the age of twenty-five and upwards, I was even more encouraged that I had served the Lord as a young man.

Indeed, it is easy to relegate the call of God to the mature and the elderly, since they seem more dignified and suitable for such responsibilities. But dear friend, dignity is not one of the fruits of the Spirit. Joy, on the other hand, which you often find in young people, is a fruit of the Spirit. I am glad I served the Lord as a young person and I would encourage you to follow the call of God in spite of your youthfulness.

9. God calls people who are *FEARFUL.*

Be not afraid of their faces: for I am with thee to deliver thee, saith the LORD.

Jeremiah 1:8

There is much to be afraid of when God calls you to the ministry. It is not unusual for you to be filled with numerous fears. The fear of the unknown is in itself a challenge. The fear of failure, ridicule and embarrassment will always make you hold back.

The fear of financial difficulty will grip your heart when you think of ministry. If you did not have any of these fears I would wonder if you were normal.

But none of these fears must keep you away from your calling. Fear is a demon. If you follow fear, you are following an evil spirit.

10. God calls people who are in *DIFFICULT CIRCUMSTANCES.*

And Gideon said unto him, Oh my Lord, *if the LORD be with us, why then is all this befallen us?* And where be all his miracles which our fathers told us of, saying, did not the LORD bring us up from Egypt? But now the LORD hath forsaken us, and delivered us into the hands of the Midianites.

Judges 6:13

Many of us want some supernatural sign that God is with us. Difficult circumstances seem to be a silent message from an invisible God that, "I am against you." If God is with us, why has all this happened to us? It is natural to ask this question. Why would God call someone He is fighting against? The circumstances may be giving a message that God is against you. But you must not allow circumstances to lead you away from your call. Circumstances are not the voice of God to you! Circumstances do have a part to play in our lives, but they are not our guiding post. We are led by the Holy Spirit; we are not led by circumstances. "For as many as are led by the Spirit of God, they are the sons of God" (Romans 8:14). Learn to hear the voice of the Spirit and trust it over and above the voice of circumstances in your life.

11. God calls people *WITHOUT MIRACLE POWER*.

And Gideon said unto him, Oh my Lord, if the LORD be with us, why then is all this befallen us? And *where be all his miracles which our fathers told us of,* saying, Did not the LORD bring us up from Egypt? But now the LORD hath forsaken us, and delivered us into the hands of the Midianites.

Judges 6:13

When God calls you, you will feel utterly powerless and "virtue-less". You will sense a strong feeling of inadequacy. One of the things you will feel is the absence of miracle and healing power in your life. Sickness has a way of telling you that God is against you. You would definitely feel like asking for miracles, signs and wonders to confirm that God is calling. If you depend on the presence of miracles to confirm your calling, you may never enter the ministry. God may have planned for you to see the first miracle after you have been in ministry for twenty years. Once again, do not depend on outward signs to know if you are called. Depend on the voice of the Holy Spirit.

12. God calls *GOD-FORSAKEN PEOPLE*.

And Gideon said unto him, Oh my Lord, if the Lord be with us, why then is all this befallen us? and where be all his miracles which our fathers told us of, saying, Did not the LORD bring us up from Egypt? But now *the Lord hath forsaken us*, and delivered us into the hands of the Midianites.

Judges 6:13

Once again, people look at their circumstances when they are responding to the call of God. They feel that their circumstances reveal whether God is with them or not. Problems and difficulties do not mean that God has forsaken you. Even if God has forsaken you, obeying the call of God will bring the presence of God back into your life. Follow the Holy Spirit into the presence of God.

13. God calls people who *HAVE NOTHING TO OFFER.*

And he said unto him, Oh my Lord, *wherewith shall I save Israel?* behold, my family is poor in Manasseh, and I am the least in my father's house.

Judges 6:15

Another reason why people do not heed the call is because they realise how little they have to offer. They do not have the Word or the anointing. They do not know much and have never accomplished anything for the Lord. Gideon asked: "What will I save the people of Israel with?" But God will teach you all that you need to know as you go along.

14. God calls people with *POOR FAMILY BACKGROUNDS.*

And he said unto him, Oh my Lord, wherewith shall I save Israel? *Behold, my family is poor in Manasseh*, and I am the least in my father's house.

Judges 6:15

Coming from a rich home boosts a person's self confidence. Riches have a way of ministering confidence because, "money answers all things." Poverty, on the other hand, fights against your self-esteem and makes you lose confidence. It is no wonder that your poverty would make you feel unworthy of the call.

Another thing that poverty does is to make you determined never to be poor. I have noticed how people from poor backgrounds have resisted the call because they want to be rich.

They want to distance themselves from the poverty of their family and their youth. Indeed, I have watched how people of poor backgrounds reject the call of God and desperately try to be rich. Sadly, many of these people fall headlong into failure.

15.   God calls people who are *THE LEAST* in their families.

And he said unto him, Oh my Lord, wherewith shall I save Israel? Behold, my family is poor in Manasseh, and *I am the least in my father's house.*

Judges 6:15

This is the usual pattern. God calls the youngest, the oddest and the rejects. Rejection has a way of making you humble. It is this humility that opens your heart to the call of God. Do not be surprised when you see the "unacceptable" person being raised up to the high office of ministry.

I remember watching an evangelist who told his father that God had told him that he would one day be an evangelist in Africa. His father was a pastor of a church. Unfortunately, his father told him, "*You* will not be my successor." Then he pointed to his oldest son and said, "He will be my successor in the ministry." This great evangelist was rejected in his own house and had a nickname "zero." The nickname, "zero" stood for a man who was unintelligent and unable to do well in school. Because he was not good in mathematics he was called a "zero." However, in spite of his father's rejection, he did become a great evangelist in Africa. Can you believe that the first son, who was chosen by his father, was not even saved at the time he was giving this testimony? Don't be worried if you are the youngest person in your family. Do not be worried if you are the least in your group. God's call will override all your natural limitations.

And Samuel said unto Jesse, Are here all thy children? And he said, *There remaineth yet the youngest,* and, behold, he keepeth the sheep. And Samuel said unto Jesse, Send and fetch him: for we will not sit down till he come hither.

1 Samuel 16:11

CHAPTER 5

What It Means to Be "Called"

Understanding what it means to be "called" will help you to obey God. Many disregard this heavenly privilege to their own hurt. To be "called" by God is a far greater privilege than to be appointed to the White House. And yet many set the "call" aside and take up other lesser opportunities. In this chapter, I want to share what it actually means to receive a "call" from God. If you understand the revelation of the "calling", you will forever appreciate your appointment. To be saved is a great privilege but to be "called" by God to work for Him in His vineyard is an incredible honour. Indeed, we do not deserve this great privilege.

1. TO BE SUMMONED DISTINCTLY

To be "called" by God means to be identified, called out by name and selected by God.

To help you further understand what a great privilege it is to be called, I want to define the concept of being called by the English, Greek and Hebrew dictionaries. The English dictionary defines the word "call" as an act in which someone is summoned distinctly. It means to be named, described, identified and labelled by God.

a. In Hebrew the word for call is *qara*, which means to call out, to properly address by name those that are bidden and called for. To be called also means to cry unto someone or to make him famous. Imagine that you reject God when He is inviting you in order to make you famous.

b. In Greek, the word for call is *kletos*, which means to be invited or appointed.

The following are examples of people who were called out by name. Indeed, it is an awesome thing that God would summon you in order to make you great and famous. There are several people whom God called by name. He mentioned their names and commanded them to obey Him. Moses, Bezaleel, Samuel, Zacchaeus and many of the disciples were called out by name. What a privilege it is to be called out by name.

And when Jesus came to the place, he looked up, and saw him, *and said unto him, Zacchaeus, make haste, and come down;* for to day I must abide at thy house.

Luke 19:5

And when the LORD saw that he turned aside to see, *God called unto him out of the midst of the bush, and said, Moses, Moses*. And he said, Here am I.

Exodus 3:4

See, *I have called by name Bezaleel* the son of Uri, the son of Hur, of the tribe of Judah:

Exodus 31:2

That *the LORD called Samuel:* and he answered, Here am I.

1 Samuel 3:4

Paul, a servant of Jesus Christ, *called to be an apostle*, separated unto the gospel of God,

Romans 1:1

And he fell to the earth, and heard a voice saying *unto him, Saul, Saul, why persecutest thou me?* And he said,

Who art thou, Lord? And the Lord said, I am Jesus whom thou persecutest: it is hard for thee to kick against the pricks.

Acts 9:4-5

Paul, ***called to be an apostle*** of Jesus Christ through the will of God, and Sosthenes our brother,

1 Corinthians 1:1

And when he had gone a little further thence, he saw James the son of Zebedee, and John his brother, who also were in the ship mending their nets. And straightway ***he called them***: and they left their father Zebedee in the ship with the hired servants, and went after him.

Mark 1:19-20

2.   RECEIVING SPECIAL MERCY

Therefore seeing we have this ministry, as ***we have received mercy,*** we faint not;

2 Corinthians 4:1

To be "called" is to receive special mercy from the Lord. To receive mercy is to experience the compassion or forbearance that is shown to an offender or an enemy. God calling you means that He is being lenient with you and is having pity on you! After salvation, the call of God to you is His greatest act of forgiveness, kindness and clemency.

a. The Hebrew word for mercy is *checed,* which refers to God showing you kindness, favour, a good deed, loving-kindness and bestowing pity on you. Indeed, for God to have called you He has shown mercy to your pitiful state.

b. The Greek word for mercy is *eleeo*, which also means to be compassionate by word or deed. This kind of mercy is something that is received by special divine grace.

3.   APPOINTED FOR A SPECIAL PURPOSE

To be "called" also means to be appointed by God for a special purpose. To be appointed by God means you have been selected for a special position. To be appointed by God also means you have been employed, signed up, assigned, selected, chosen and picked for the job. Why then would you allow yourself to be employed by someone lesser than Almighty God Himself?

a. In Hebrew, to be appointed *(paqad)* means to give a charge to someone or set him over something. It also means to commit something to someone and to give him the oversight of it. What a privilege it is to have received such an appointment!

b. The Greek word for "appoint" is *diatithemai*, which means to give someone an assignment. Your life on this earth is an assignment and you have to complete this assignment at all costs.

> ***But thou shalt appoint the Levites*** over the tabernacle of testimony, and over all the vessels thereof, and over all things that belong to it: they shall bear the tabernacle, and all the vessels thereof; and they shall minister unto it, and shall encamp round about the tabernacle.
>
> Numbers 1:50

> And ***thou shalt appoint Aaron and his sons,*** and they shall wait on their priest's office: and the stranger that cometh nigh shall be put to death.
>
> Numbers 3:10

> And David said unto Michal, It was before the LORD, which chose me before thy father, and before all his house, ***to appoint me ruler over the people*** of the LORD, over Israel: therefore will I play before the LORD.
>
> 2 Samuel 6:21

> And David spake to the chief of the Levites to appoint their brethren to be the singers with instruments of musick, psalteries and harps and cymbals, sounding, by lifting up the voice with joy.
> ***So the Levites appointed Heman*** the son of Joel; and of his brethren, Asaph the son of Berechiah; and of the sons

of Merari their brethren, Ethan the son of Kushaiah; and
with them their brethren of the second degree, Zechariah,
Ben, and Jaaziel, and Shemiramoth, and Jehiel, and Unni,
Eliab, and Benaiah, and Maaseiah, and Mattithiah, and
Elipheleh, and Mikneiah, and Obed-edom, and Jeiel, the
porters.

So the singers, Heman, Asaph, and Ethan, were appointed
to sound with cymbals of brass;

1 Chronicles 15:16-19

4.   SEPARATED FOR GOD'S PURPOSES

To be "called" by God means to be separated for His purposes.
Perhaps, this is the most important definition of what it means
to be "called".   God's calling isolates you and separates you
from the larger body of Christians.   To be separated means to
detach somebody or something from a larger group.   Your calling
therefore means that you have been isolated for the purposes of
God.

Your calling means you have been separated from the larger
society of lay Christians. Separation speaks of being severed
from an association.   This separation also means that you have
been withdrawn from something.   In this case, you have been
withdrawn from secular life and secular ideals.   By your calling,
you have also been separated from your family and friends.
Indeed, a high calling even means that you have been separated
from other Christians.

a. The Hebrew word for separate is *badal*, which means to
    distinguish and make a difference between you and others.
    Is it not a blessing that God has distinguished between you
    and others?   He has made a difference between you and
    other believers! What else can you ask for?

b. The Greek word for separate is *aphorizo*, which also means
    to keep apart two or more people or things by a boundary.
    God is keeping you apart and has put a boundary between
    you and the rest.   What higher blessing could you hope for
    than for God to keep you apart for His special purposes?

At that time *the LORD separated the tribe of Levi*, to bear the ark of the covenant of the LORD, to stand before the LORD to minister unto him, and to bless in his name, unto this day.

Deuteronomy 10:8

When the most High divided to the nations their inheritance, when *he separated the sons of Adam*, he set the bounds of the people according to the number of the children of Israel.

Deuteronomy 32:8

The sons of Amram; Aaron and Moses: and *Aaron was separated*, that he should sanctify the most holy things, he and his sons for ever, to burn incense before the LORD, to minister unto him, and to bless in his name for ever.

1 Chronicles 23:13

Paul, a servant of Jesus Christ, called to be an apostle, *separated unto the gospel of God*,

Romans 1:1

But when it pleased God, who *separated me from my mother's womb*, and called me by his grace,

Galatians 1:15

As they ministered to the Lord, and fasted, the Holy Ghost said, *Separate me Barnabas and Saul* for the work whereunto I have called them.

Acts 13:2

5. TO BE SENT OUT PROPERLY

To be "called" by God means to be sent out. There is a difference between someone who was sent and someone who just went! God sending you means He is dispatching you on a journey to serve Him or to get something for Him. Indeed, God is sending you to fetch many souls from the grips of the devil.

a. The Hebrew word for "sent" is *shalach,* which means to send someone away. The call of God often means that you will be sent away from your family and friends.

b. In the Greek, the word "sent" is *apostello*, which means to set someone apart and to send someone out properly on a mission. Many people are not sent out properly and this affects their entire ministry. You must strive to be sent out properly, because one day your authority will be challenged. Jesus was asked by which authority He was doing the things He did. John Wesley was challenged about who sent and authorised him. John Wesley simply told them that the Archbishop of Canterbury had ordained him. It is out of order to minister without being sent out properly. Indeed, every minister must strive to be ordained and sent out properly. It is this "proper" sending that ensures a blessing on the work you do.

And ***God sent me before you to preserve you*** a posterity in the earth, and to save your lives by a great deliverance.

Genesis 45:7

And God said moreover unto Moses, Thus shalt thou say unto the children of Israel, The LORD God of your fathers, the God of Abraham, the God of Isaac, and ***the God of Jacob***, ***hath sent me unto you***: this is my name for ever, and this is my memorial unto all generations.

Exodus 3:15

But the LORD said unto me, Say not, I am a child: ***for thou shalt go to all that I shall send thee***, and whatsoever I command thee thou shalt speak.

Jeremiah 1:7

For thus saith the LORD of hosts; ***after the glory hath he sent me*** unto the nations which spoiled you: for he that toucheth you toucheth the apple of his eye.

Zechariah 2:8

The Spirit of the Lord is upon me, because he hath anointed me to preach the gospel to the poor; *he hath sent me to heal the brokenhearted,* to preach deliverance to the captives, and recovering of sight to the blind, to set at liberty them that are bruised,

Luke 4:18

There was a man sent from God, whose name was John.

John 1:6

Jesus saith unto them, *my meat is to do the will of him that sent me*, and to finish his work.

John 4:34

6.   RECEIVING GRACE FROM GOD

To be "called" by God means that the grace of God is upon you. In the first place, it is God's unmerited favour that gives us our salvation. But when God calls you, He shows you even *more* kindness and clemency. This kindness is over and above the kindness that caused your salvation.

As you can see, it is when this unmerited favour is extended even further that you receive a call to work for God! Indeed, to receive grace is to receive favour, benevolence, clemency and leniency. It is this leniency from God that invites and welcomes somebody like you into the ministry!

a. The Hebrew word for "grace" is *chen*, which means graciousness, kindness, receiving favour or becoming precious. From this definition, receiving a call and receiving grace means that you have been well-favoured by the Lord. Indeed, you are precious because the call of God is upon you.

b. The Greek word for "grace" is *charis*, which speaks of the divine influence upon your heart. This grace will only stir up gratitude that motivates you.

And the child grew, and waxed strong in spirit, filled with wisdom: and *the grace of God was upon him*.

Luke 2:40

And the Word was made flesh, and dwelt among us, (and we beheld his glory, the glory as of the only begotten of the Father,) *full of grace* and truth.

John 1:14

For I say, *through the grace given unto me*, to every man that is among you, not to think of himself more highly than he ought to think; but to think soberly, according as God hath dealt to every man the measure of faith.

Romans 12:3

Having then gifts differing *according to the grace that is given to us,* whether prophecy, let us prophesy according to the proportion of faith;

Romans 12:6

There is one body, and one Spirit, even as ye are called in one hope of your calling; one Lord, one faith, one baptism, one God and Father of all, who is above all, and through all, and in you all. But *unto every one of us is given grace* according to the measure of the gift of Christ.

Ephesians 4:4-7

7. RECEIVING A MINISTRY FROM GOD

To be "called" by God means you have received a ministry from God. To receive a ministry from God is to come into possession of the duties and functions of a particular stream of Kingdom work. What a blessing to be welcomed into the functions of a particular line of God's work. When you are called, God welcomes your special line of service to Him.

a. The Hebrew word for "ministry" is *yad*, which refers to service in the Temple.

b. The Greek word for "ministry" is *diakonia,* which speaks of the service of the Christian.

And say to Archippus, ***Take heed to the ministry which thou hast received*** in the Lord, that thou fulfil it.

Colossians 4:17

I beseech you, brethren, (ye know the house of Stephanas, that it is the firstfruits of Achaia, and that ***they have addicted themselves to the ministry of the saints,***)

1 Corinthians 16:15

And all things are of God, who hath reconciled us to himself by Jesus Christ, and ***hath given to us the ministry of reconciliation;***

2 Corinthians 5:18

Or ministry, let us wait on our ministering: or he that teacheth, on teaching;

Romans 12:7

8. RECEIVING A TALENT FROM GOD

For the kingdom of heaven is as a man travelling into a far country, who called his own servants, and delivered unto them his goods. And unto one he gave *five talents,* to another two, and to another one; to every man according to his several ability; and straightway took his journey.

Matthew 25:14-15

To be "called" by God is to receive a talent from God. A talent is a gift, a capacity, ability or an endowment from God. God expects you to use this tangible endowment to advance the Kingdom. A talent can also be described as a general ability or some specific intelligence given to you by God. Receiving a talent speaks of receiving a special creative aptitude. When you are called, you receive a flair for doing certain things.

a. The Hebrew word for "talent" is *kikkar,* which is a round loaf, a morsel, a piece or a large round coin. These speak of something tangible that can be used to serve God. God has put something tangible in your hands and He expects you to accomplish something with it.

b. The Greek word for "talent" is *talanton* and speaks of a weight used for a balance. Once again, it signifies something tangible you have been given to use.

9. RECEIVING A GIFT FROM GOD

To be called by God means you have received a gift from God. This gift is a natural capacity or talent freely given to you by God. To be called by God is to be given a natural capacity for certain things. This is why people who are called seem to do certain things effortlessly. If you are called to pastor a church, you will have the gift of effortlessly looking after troublesome people for many years. If you are called to evangelize you will have the gift of loving the poor masses who have nothing to give in return.

a. The Hebrew word for "gift" is *mattan*, which means a present.

b. The Greek word for "gift" is *charisma*, which means a gratuity, a spiritual endowment or a religious qualification.

For I long to see you, ***that I may impart unto you some spiritual gift***, to the end ye may be established;

Romans 1:11

Having then gifts differing according to the grace that is given to us, whether prophecy, let us prophesy according to the proportion of faith;

Romans 12:6

Follow after charity, and ***desire spiritual gifts,*** but rather that ye may prophesy.

1 Corinthians 14:1

Neglect not the gift that is in thee, which was given thee by prophecy, with the laying on of the hands of the presbytery.

1 Timothy 4:14

Wherefore I put thee in remembrance that thou *stir up the gift of God*, which is in thee by the putting on of my hands.

2 Timothy 1:6

10. RECEIVING AN OFFICE

To be "called" by God means you have received an office. What a blessing this is! To be called by God is to be put in an office by the Lord. What greater privilege can you have than to be given an office by the Lord? An "office" is a place of work, a responsibility, a job, a position, a task and a function. Anyone who is called has received an office with special responsibilities. Your new and special office gives you a position of authority or power. Indeed, to be called is to receive an office from God and to come into possession of a position which gives you much authority.

a. The Hebrew word for "office", *ma`amad* also speaks of a position and office that you have received.

b. The Greek word for "office" is *praxis*, which refers to what has become your new function and practice.

And this is the thing that thou shalt do unto them to hallow them, *to minister unto me in the priest's office*: Take one young bullock, and two rams without blemish,

Exodus 29:1

All these which were chosen to be porters in the gates were two hundred and twelve. These were reckoned by their genealogy in their villages, whom David and *Samuel the seer did ordain in their set office*.

1 Chronicles 9:22

41

Because their office was to wait on the sons of Aaron for the service of the house of the LORD, in the courts, and in the chambers, and in the purifying of all holy things, and the work of the service of the house of God;

1 Chronicles 23:28

And I made treasurers over the treasuries, Shelemiah the priest, and Zadok the scribe, and of the Levites, Pedaiah: and next to them was Hanan the son of Zaccur, the son of Mattaniah: for they were counted faithful, and ***their office was to distribute unto their brethren***.

Nehemiah 13:13

For I speak to you Gentiles, inasmuch as I am the apostle of the Gentiles, ***I magnify mine office***:

Romans 11:13

For as we have many members in one body, and ***all members have not the same office***:

Romans 12:4

And let these also first be proved; then ***let them use the office of a deacon,*** being found blameless.

1 Timothy 3:10

CHAPTER 6

The Limitations of an Individual's Calling

1. We have only a "measure" of a call.

Human beings long to create super-human characters who never make mistakes, never fail and never die. It is this inward desire in all men that has created characters like James Bond, Rambo, Superman, Demolition man, Batman and Spiderman, etc. But the fact that you are "called" will not turn you into any of these super-human characters. Your calling is simply God showing mercy and leniency to you. Apart from this, your calling is limited. You have received only a measure of the Spirit. "But unto every one of us is given grace according to the measure of the gift of Christ" (Ephesians 4:7).

Your calling gives you only a measure of the Spirit and there are several other measures you did not receive. This means that there are several other gifts that you lack. Your lack of other graces will always limit you in the ministry. Your lack of other gifts will prevent you from being successful in certain fields. God has reserved those fields of ministry for others.

It is because they have just a measure of the Spirit. This fact alone forces ministers to be humble in spite of how greatly they are gifted. Notice how these Scriptures emphasize the reality of us receiving just a portion and not the whole thing.

Only Christ received the full measure of the Spirit. "For he whom God hath sent speaketh the words of God: for God giveth not the Spirit by measure unto him" (John 3:34). You and I have just a measure of the Spirit.

> And OF HIS FULNESS HAVE ALL WE RECEIVED, and grace for grace.
>
> John 1:16

> For I say, through the grace given unto me, to every man that is among you, not to think of himself more highly than he ought to think; but to think soberly, according as God hath dealt TO EVERY MAN THE MEASURE OF FAITH.
>
> Romans 12:3

> Till we all come in the unity of the faith, and of the knowledge of the Son of God, unto a perfect man, UNTO THE MEASURE OF THE STATURE OF THE FULNESS OF CHRIST:
>
> Ephesians 4:13

> But all these worketh that one and the selfsame Spirit, DIVIDING TO EVERY MAN SEVERALLY AS HE WILL.
>
> 1 Corinthians 12:11

2. Only Christ has the fullness of the call.

> **For IN HIM DWELLETH ALL THE FULNESS of the Godhead bodily.**
>
> **Colossians 2:9**

If you want to see the fullness of the call, you must look at Christ since only Christ has the ultimate calling. This is a very important truth for us to grasp. You must make Christ your best example of a shepherd, a teacher, an evangelist and a prophet. Constantly looking at Christ will cause you to move much higher than you would have been. Unfortunately, many of us look at men we esteem as mentors and assume they are the best example of ministry.

I often have this difficulty of seeing people as having only "a measure". I often cannot imagine anything better than what I see. But I have had to accept the fact that even the most anointed men of God are only a measure of what they could be. Every one of us is only a fraction of what we could be if we had the full measure of the gift. It is Christ who had the Spirit without measure and therefore is the fullest and the best example of ministry.

3.   You must not look to any man as the ultimate minister.

The ultimate pastor is the good shepherd, Jesus Christ. The ultimate teacher is Jesus Christ. The ultimate evangelist was the Lord who came to seek and to save the lost. The ultimate prophet was Jesus, the prophet, whose words have never failed. The ultimate apostle was Jesus who was sent by God as the Saviour of the world.

4.   You must recognize the limitations of people you look up to without despising them.

Inasmuch as you are to see that people are limited, you must not despise them for their limitations. It is important not to idolize anyone but it is also important not to despise them. Most people despise and criticise men of God because they see the non-gifted, raw aspects of these men. Indeed, it is very easy to despise a man of God. In one field he looks invincible yet in another he seems to be almost an imbecile. Learn to recognize the grace of God. Seeing the weakness of someone who is called should make you appreciate the grace of God even more. "Stop regarding man, whose breath of life is in his nostrils; for why should he be esteemed?" (Isaiah 2:22, NASB).

5.   You must recognize your own limitations in ministry.

Unfortunately, recognizing your own limitations can be extremely difficult. People rarely accept that they cannot do certain things. People rarely accept criticisms about their person or their ability. This is proved by Proverbs 21:2: "Every man's way is right in his own eyes..." (NASB).

But perhaps the hallmark of the greatest men of God is the ability to see where the gift ends and the natural takes over. The apostle Paul knew when he was outside the grace and the revelation. He often stated when he was speaking his own mind and when he was sharing from the gift he had received. For example Paul said, "Now concerning virgins I have no commandment of the Lord: yet I give my judgment, as one that hath obtained mercy of the Lord to be faithful" (1 Corinthians 7:25).

This is rare. Most prophets want to extend their powers and become like super men and almighty magicians. But we are limited and we are not magicians. Even though you are called you will be limited and time will prove this.

6.   You must be humble because you do not have it all.

It is wonderful to see people so gifted in one area and almost dim-witted in another. Christ is the only one who receives the anointing without measure and is the only one who needs no inputs from anyone. All of us have received a measure and do not have anything in full. This makes us need others in order to be complete. It also makes us have to relate with others whom we may have otherwise despised. This is part of God's wonderful plan to make us the humble children we must be.

7.   Your limitations in ministry are overcome by recognizing the contribution of others to your life.

There will be other people who know more about certain areas of ministry. It is important that you humble yourself to receive God's blessings from them. Learn from pastors with bigger churches and learn from pastors with smaller churches. God's power is real and He will send people to help you become who you must become. Every joint will supply something until you have become what God has called you to be. "From whom the whole body fitly joined together and compacted by that which EVERY JOINT SUPPLIETH, according to the effectual working in the measure of every part, maketh increase of the body unto the edifying of itself in love" (Ephesians 4:16). Every joint is supplying something that you need for your life and ministry.

CHAPTER 7

What is in Your Heart?

Love not the world, neither the things that are in the world. If any man loves the world, the love of the Father is not in him.

1 John 2:15

Many Christians have fallen in love with the world rather than falling in love with Christ. It is important to allow your heart to be filled with Christ. How can we know what is in our hearts? By the things we say! Out of the abundance of the heart the mouth speaks. Out of the abundance of the hearts of the pastors you hear them speak and preach. What do you mostly hear about? We often hear about money, prosperity, success, etc. These things have filled our hearts. The love of the world is in our hearts and the love for the things in the world is also in our hearts.

Today, Jesus is standing at the door of the hearts of all Christians, knocking and asking to be let in. He wants to take His rightful place. He wants to drive away all illegal occupants who have no right to be in the hearts of His children.

> **Behold, I stand at the door, and knock: if any man hear my voice, and open the door, I will come in to him, and will sup with him, and he with me.**
>
> **Revelation 3:20**

This Scripture is used commonly by evangelists who are trying to persuade people to open their hearts to Jesus Christ. Surprisingly, this Scripture has nothing to do with salvation and conversion. It is a letter to the church, which has Jesus Christ standing outside and asking to be let in. How come Jesus is standing outside His own church? What is the reason for Christ not being welcomed to His own body?

Margaret

I once heard this story of a lady called Margaret. During the Second World War, many young Germans were forced to join the army to fight for their country. There was a young lady called Margaret who had just been married to this handsome young soldier. Unfortunately, shortly after their marriage he had to leave for the battlefield. In great sadness he wept over his new bride Margaret and kissed her a hundred times. He said "bye bye" to her and left for the war.

He dearly wanted to come back to his beautiful bride Margaret. Unfortunately, he was sent to the front lines and was captured almost immediately by the Russian army. He thus became a Russian prisoner of war and was sent to work in the camps. In the prison, he prayed constantly that he would be released so that he could go back to his beautiful bride, Margaret. Being a prisoner of war was a terrible experience. He suffered very much and was subjected to the hard labour of a prisoner of war. Every day, when he got up, he would think of Margaret! In every step he made during the day, carrying rocks and boulders from place to place; in the cold and in the heat, he thought of only one thing – Margaret!

The years went by and Germany lost the war. The prisoners were excited because they hoped to be released alive. One day the commander of the prisoners of war came up with a list of prisoners who were to be released. This young soldier was excited because he thought he would be released. Unfortunately, when the names were read out, his name was not on the list. His hopes were dashed! He was greatly disappointed and his heart sank. He had lost the chance to see Margaret.

But the very next week, another list of prisoners to be released was read out by the commander of the prison and this young soldier's name was on the list. What a day of rejoicing that was! He could think of only one thing – Margaret! "I am going to see Margaret!" He packed his few belongings and took a train to Germany to see his beloved Margaret!

Through every step of that long journey he thought of only one thing – Margaret! When he finally arrived in his town he was shocked to find that almost every building had been bombed and the town that he once knew was basically a pile of rubble. He walked down the street and came to the road where he had lived with Margaret.

To his amazement, their house was one of the few still standing. His heart began to beat as he walked up to the door. The moment of truth had come. He knocked on the door and waited in silence, wondering if anybody lived in that house. Suddenly, he heard footsteps, which he recognized. "These are the footsteps of Margaret," he thought.

Suddenly the door opened and there she was; more beautiful than the noonday sun, more splendid than she had looked on her wedding day! The young soldier lifted up his hands and screamed, "Margaret, I am back!"

Suddenly, something terrible happened. Margaret slammed the door and locked it. The young soldier was shocked.

He began knocking and banging on the door, "Margaret, Margaret, I am your husband. Open the door! Margaret, Margaret, I am your husband. Open the door!"

But she did not open the door. He could not believe what was happening. Why was Margaret not opening the door? This young man who had looked forward to seeing his beautiful bride was now in a state of shock. He stood outside the door knocking and calling for Margaret but she simply did not open the door.

Do You Want to Know Why?

Do you want to know why Margaret did not open the door? I will tell you why. It is the same reason why the church is not opening the door of its heart to Jesus. There was somebody else in the house! That is why Margaret did not open the door! Another man had come to live in the house whilst Margaret's husband was away at war. *Something* and *someone* else was in there and the rightful owner was on the outside begging.

Jesus is equally standing at the door of the heart of the church today, asking to be let in to take His rightful place. Unfortunately, other things are in there and that is why Jesus is on the outside.

The love for the world has filled the heart of the church and Jesus is outside knocking and asking to be let in.

Money, wealth, and the deceitfulness of them all, have possessed the pulpit and the pew alike. No wonder Jesus is asking to be let back into His wealthy, last-day church! Satan has crept in and occupied the chair that he has no right to.

If Jesus occupies our hearts, we will be filled with the knowledge of His will and be in love with Him and not with the world. It is sad that our hearts have gone after earthly and worldly things. It is indeed pathetic that mammon has been welcomed into the church and has replaced Christ. We are richer than we have ever been but if Christ is outside then our riches will become a snare to us. "But lusted exceedingly in the wilderness, and tempted God in the desert. And he gave them their request; but sent leanness into their soul" (Psalm 106:14-15).

CHAPTER 8

How God Monitors Your Works

God never said He was keeping an eye on your cars and houses. Yet Christians today are engrossed in numerous activities to create more earthly treasures for themselves. Most of these things have no eternal value. We assess people by their clothes and jewellery. We assess people by their homes. We assess people by the cars they drive. But Jesus said, "You shall know them by their fruits." Jesus did not say you shall know them by their car or their houses.

God is not against these things but that is *not* what God is monitoring. God's eyes are on your *works*! God is watching the labour and effort that you are putting in for the sake of His kingdom. If you do not have any such "works", eternity will hold the greatest shock for your life! You will notice from the Scriptures below that the phrase, "I know your works" is mentioned repeatedly.

Every one of the seven churches in the book of Revelation is told the same thing. God knows the works you have done! God is watching your works! God has His eye on the things you are doing for His kingdom!

The letters to the seven churches serve as a revelation of our future judgement when we stand before God. We now know what we will be assessed about. This is the best "past question" that we could ever have.

Seven Times God Said, "I Know Your Works"

1. **Ephesus, I know your works.**

   Unto the angel of the church of Ephesus … I KNOW THY WORKS, and thy labour, and thy patience, and how thou canst not bear them which are evil: and thou hast tried them which say they are apostles, and are not, and hast found them liars: And hast borne, and hast patience, and for my name's sake hast laboured, and hast not fainted.

   Revelation 2:1-3

2. **Smyrna, I know your works.**

   And unto the angel of the church in Smyrna write; These things saith the first and the last, which was dead, and is alive; I KNOW THY WORKS, and tribulation, and poverty, (but thou art rich) and I know the blasphemy of them which say they are Jews, and are not, but are the synagogue of Satan. Fear none of those things which thou shalt suffer: behold, the devil shall cast some of you into prison, that ye may be tried; and ye shall have tribulation ten days: be thou faithful unto death, and I will give thee a crown of life.

   Revelation 2:8-10

3. **Pergamos, I know your works.**

   And to the angel of the church in Pergamos write; These things saith he which hath the sharp sword with two edges; I KNOW THY WORKS, and where thou dwellest, even where Satan's seat is: and thou holdest fast my name, and hast not denied my faith, even in those days wherein Antipas was my faithful martyr, who was slain among you, where Satan dwelleth. But I have a few things against thee, because thou hast there them that hold the doctrine of Balaam, who taught Balac to cast a stumblingblock before the children of Israel, to eat things sacrificed unto idols, and to commit fornication.

Revelation 2:12-14

4.   Thyatira, I know your works.

And unto the angel of the church in Thyatira write; These things saith the Son of God, who hath his eyes like unto a flame of fire, and his feet are like fine brass;

I KNOW THY WORKS, and charity, and service, and faith, and thy patience, and thy works; and the last to be more than the first. Notwithstanding I have a few things against thee, because thou sufferest that woman Jezebel, which calleth herself a prophetess, to teach and to seduce my servants to commit fornication, and to eat things sacrificed unto idols.

Revelation 2:18-20

5.   Sardis, I know your works.

And unto the angel of the church in Sardis write; These things saith he that hath the seven Spirits of God, and the seven stars; I KNOW THY WORKS, that thou hast a name that thou livest, and art dead. Be watchful, and strengthen the things which remain, that are ready to die: for I have not found thy works perfect before God. Remember therefore how thou hast received and heard, and hold fast, and repent. If therefore thou shalt not watch, I will come on thee as a thief, and thou shalt not know what hour I will come upon thee.

Revelation 3:1-3

6.   Philadelphia, I know your works.

And to the angel of the church in Philadelphia write; These things saith he that is holy, he that is true, he that hath the key of David, he that openeth, and no man shutteth; and shutteth, and no man openeth; I KNOW THY WORKS:

55

behold, I have set before thee an open door, and no man can shut it: for thou hast a little strength, and hast kept my word, and hast not denied my name.

Revelation 3:7-8

7. Laodiceans, I know your works.

And unto the angel of the church of the Laodiceans write; These things saith the Amen, the faithful and true witness, the beginning of the creation of God; I KNOW THY WORKS, that thou art neither cold nor hot: I would thou wert cold or hot.

So then because thou art lukewarm, and neither cold nor hot, I will spue thee out of my mouth. Because thou sayest, I am rich, and increased with goods, and have need of nothing; and knowest not that thou art wretched, and miserable, and poor, and blind, and naked:

Revelation 3:14-17

CHAPTER 9

Barren Because You Are Blind to Hell

For if these things be in you, and abound, they make you that ye shall neither be barren nor unfruitful in the knowledge of our Lord Jesus Christ. But he that lacketh these things is BLIND, and cannot see afar off, and hath forgotten that he was purged from his old sins.

2 Peter 1:8-9

Why Many Christians Are Fruitless

Unable to See Hell

The inability to see the reality of Hell is a cause for much of the prevailing barrenness in Christian circles. Moses pleased God because he saw the invisible. "By faith he forsook Egypt, not fearing the wrath of the king: for he endured, as seeing him who is invisible" (Hebrews 11:27).

Jesus Christ Was Not Blind

He had His eyes on Heaven and Hell throughout His ministry. To say that Jesus Christ spoke more about money than anything else is a misrepresentation of Christ and His message. The spirit of Christ's message was to point us towards eternity. He came to teach us about the eternal God who dwells in Heaven above. He taught us about the reality of eternal judgement.

Blindness to Hell

Jesus told us about Lazarus and the rich man. If this story is true (and it is) then it is worth giving up everything and going to the rest of the world to tell them about Jesus. I want you to remember these facts about Lazarus and the rich man.

Fifteen Lessons from Lazarus and the Rich Man

1. This was not a parable because Jesus mentioned the name of Lazarus, who must have been a real person who once existed in their town. This frightening story is the most reliable account of life after death given to mankind. *Most preachers do not read it nor preach from it. Consequently, the church is shielded from visions of Hell*. This causes blindness as far as eternity is concerned. And it is this blindness that leads to passivity and barrenness.

2. The poor man died before the rich man because the poor usually die before the rich. This is simply a pattern on this earth. However, the rich man went to Hell and the poor man went to heaven. *This shows that living long does not make you go to a good place when you die*.

3. From the story of Lazarus and the rich man, *we know that there is, at least, one rich man in Hell. This implies that there could be several other rich men in Hell.* This must be a warning to all rich men.

4. The rich man had a luxurious life; clothed in purple and fine linen, faring sumptuously every day. In spite of this, the rich man went to Hell and the poor man went to Heaven.

   This shows that no matter how rich and luxurious your life is, you can be thrown into Hell. This is a very frightening thought for those who have only known luxury and wealth on earth.

   When I saw the trials of multi-millionaires like Michael Jackson and the Chief Executive of Enron who were on trial for various alleged crimes I realized how the richest men on earth could be in danger of being thrown into horrible prisons with dangerous criminals. If human beings can do this to the rich men on earth, then Almighty God can, and will throw rich men who do not fear Him into Hell.

5. The poor man suffered greatly and had dogs dressing his sores on a daily basis. They licked up the blood and the puss that exuded from the huge ulcers on his legs. Yet, when this poor man died, he found his place in Abraham's bosom. *This shows us that God loves humble and poor people even if we don't.* Unlike most Christians, who often shun these people, Jesus loved them and He died for them. It is no wonder that it is often poor people who believe the stories of Heaven and Hell.

6. *When poor Lazarus died, he was carried by angels into Abraham's bosom.* This is important to know because evil spirits that inhabit this world would love to capture every

soul that is freed from the body and take it to Hell. That is why a heavenly escort of angels is necessary upon the death of a saint.

7. ***When the rich man died, he also had a welcoming reception party.*** Jesus did not tell us anything more than that the rich man descended. But Isaiah says "Hell from beneath is moved for thee to meet thee at thy coming..." (Isaiah 14:9).

8. Another important point to note is the fact that the rich man saw and recognized Lazarus in Abraham's bosom. ***This fact shows that we will continue our lives after this world and be able to recognize one another over in the new world.*** In the next world, you will recognize anyone you knew on earth. This is why the rich man recognized Lazarus. He remembered the gate of his big house on earth. He also remembered the beggar at his gate.

9. ***This story brings alive the reality of an inner, inward or hidden man.*** There is a man inside the physical body we inhabit. It is this hidden man who lives on when the body dies. The inner man is the spirit and soul of a human being. The spirit of a man is not a breeze wafting along or a pocket of wind that can be blown away. The spirit of a man is actually a man.

For which cause we faint not; but though our outward man perish, yet the inward man is renewed day by day.
2 Corinthians 4:16

That he would grant you, according to the riches of his glory, to be strengthened with might by his Spirit in the inner man;
Ephesians 3:16

But let it be the hidden man of the heart, in that which is not corruptible, even the ornament of a meek and quiet spirit, which is in the sight of God of great price.
1 Peter 3:4

In this story, when the rich man died, he asked for Lazarus to dip the tip of his finger into water and cool his tongue. A finger is attached to a hand, which is attached to the body. A tongue is attached to the mouth, which is in the head. As you can see, Jesus was describing the body of a man. This shows that our spirits are actually inner, inward or hidden men. You are not a waft of air. You are a man living inside the body of a man!

10. There is a place where the worm dieth not and where the fire is not quenched. *In this place called Hell, people seek just a drop of water to alleviate their indescribable constant suffering.* The torment of the rich man must be understood to be something beyond human comprehension. There are many experiences of suffering that people have but this description beats them all. He asked for a drop of water. In all my life I have never met anyone who asked for just a drop of water. People always ask for a glass of water or a bottle of water!

11. *The ability to remember your life on earth is something that will add to the experience of Heaven or Hell.* Abraham told the rich man to remember his life on earth. "But Abraham said, SON, REMEMBER that thou in thy lifetime receivedst thy good things, and likewise Lazarus evil things: but now he is comforted, and thou art tormented" (Luke 16:25).

12. One of the saddest facts that Jesus wanted us to know was that *we would not be able to change our location once we ended up in Hell.* Jesus spoke in detail about how there was a great chasm that separated Heaven and Hell making it impossible for transfers or visits. Where you "land" is where you will stay forever.

13. One amazing fact is that the rich man was very concerned about his relatives not coming to that place. *It seems that when a man descends into Hell he has no other concern than that others should not join him there.* This great concern of the rich man for his lost family is interesting,

because many Christians, and even pastors, on earth do not show any concern for the lost. They preach and teach for happy family lives, prosperity and success. These are good topics, but the rich man in Hell didn't seem to want his family to have any of these things. *He just did not want them to come to Hell.*

Why don't we have the same passion for the lost as this rich unbeliever had when he went to Hell? I challenge you to believe in the reality of Hell whilst you are on earth. I challenge you to preach about it as though you have seen it. I challenge you to stop being silent on this important topic. I challenge you to make it a vision that is before your eyes all the time. It will galvanize you into fruitfulness. *If some rich people in our churches would have the experience of going to Hell and back, they would finance evangelism with all their strength and wealth.*

14. ***The rich man then exposed one of the common mistakes of unsaved people: Wanting some dramatic experience to challenge them into repentance.*** The rich man wanted Lazarus to rise from the dead and go speak to his brothers. Abraham knew better; if they did not listen to preachers they would not listen to someone who had risen from the dead. In fact, they would be the first to ridicule any stories about someone rising from the dead. They would accuse people of being dim-witted, superstitious, ignorant, stupid and unintelligent. They would accuse pastors of being brainless for believing in something as far-fetched as people rising from the dead.

15. ***God has chosen that people should be saved by preaching.*** Abraham told the rich man that his brothers would have to listen to Moses and the other prophets who were preaching all the time. "...It pleased God by the foolishness of preaching to save them that believe" (1 Corinthians 1:21).

CHAPTER 10

Barren Because You Are Blind to Heaven

For if these things be in you, and abound, they make you that ye shall neither be barren nor unfruitful in the knowledge of our Lord Jesus Christ. But he that lacketh these things is BLIND, and cannot see afar off, and hath forgotten that he was purged from his old sins.

2 Peter 1:8-9

Can You See Heaven?
Do You Have Another World in View?

Christians have become barren because they do not have another world in view. All we have in view are our new cars, houses, money and other earthly possessions. Not having another world in view means you cannot see Heaven or Hell. It means that the existence of another world is not impressed on your heart. Christians must see the other world of Heaven and this will motivate them to work for God. We must have another world in view!

> **If ye then be risen with Christ, seek those things which are above, where Christ sitteth on the right hand of God. Set your affection on things above, not on things on the earth.**
>
> **Colossians 3:1-2**

Jesus saw Heaven and spoke constantly of His heavenly Father. Jesus constantly spoke of Heaven. He spoke of a place that He was going to. He did not speak of this earth as a place to live forever. He spoke passionately of Heaven and how He was on His way there. Jesus constantly spoke of going away from this earth. He spoke of going to some other place. He also spoke of a place that He had come from. He clearly seemed to have another world in view.

Fifteen Times Jesus Had
Another World in View

1. Then said Jesus unto them, yet a little while am I with you, and then I GO UNTO HIM THAT SENT ME.

   John 7:33

2. Jesus answered and said unto them, though I bear record of myself, yet my record is true: FOR I KNOW WHENCE I CAME, AND WHITHER I GO; but ye cannot tell whence I come, and whither I go.

   John 8:14

3.   Then said Jesus again unto them, I GO MY WAY, and ye shall seek me, and shall die in your sins: WHITHER I GO, YE CANNOT COME. Then said the Jews, Will he kill himself? because he saith, Whither I go, ye cannot come.

John 8:21-22

4.   Little children, yet a little while I am with you. Ye shall seek me: and as I said unto the Jews, WHITHER I GO, YE CANNOT COME; so now I say to you.

John 13:33

5.   Simon Peter said unto him, Lord, whither goest thou? Jesus answered him, WHITHER I GO, THOU CANST NOT FOLLOW ME NOW; BUT THOU SHALT FOLLOW ME AFTERWARDS.

John 13:36

6.   In my Father's house are many mansions: if it were not so, I would have told you. I GO TO PREPARE A PLACE FOR YOU. And if I go and prepare a place for you, I will come again, and receive you unto myself; that where I am, there ye may be also. And whither I go ye know, and the way ye know.

John 14:2-3

7.   Verily, verily, I say unto you, He that believeth on me, the works that I do shall he do also; and greater works than these shall he do; because I GO UNTO MY FATHER.

John 14:12

8.   YE HAVE HEARD HOW I SAID UNTO YOU, I GO AWAY, AND COME AGAIN UNTO YOU. If ye loved me, ye would rejoice, because I said, I go unto the Father: for my Father is greater than I.

John 14:28

9.   BUT NOW I GO MY WAY TO HIM THAT SENT ME; and none of you asketh me, Whither goest thou?

John 16:5

10. Nevertheless I tell you the truth; IT IS EXPEDIENT FOR YOU THAT I GO AWAY: for if I go not away, the Comforter will not come unto you; but if I depart, I will send him unto you.

John 16:7

11. Of righteousness, BECAUSE I GO TO MY FATHER, and ye see me no more;

John 16:10

12. A LITTLE WHILE, AND YE SHALL NOT SEE ME: AND AGAIN, A LITTLE WHILE, AND YE SHALL SEE ME, BECAUSE I GO TO THE FATHER.

Then said some of his disciples among themselves, What is this that he saith unto us, A little while, and ye shall not see me: and again, a little while, and ye shall see me: and, Because I go to the Father?

John 16:16-17

13. I came forth from the Father, and am come into the world: again, I LEAVE THE WORLD, AND GO TO THE FATHER.

John 16:28

14. AND THEN SHALL APPEAR THE SIGN OF THE SON OF MAN IN HEAVEN: and then shall all the tribes of the earth mourn, and they shall see the Son of man coming in the clouds of heaven with power and great glory.

Matthew 24:30

15. Jesus saith unto him, Thou hast said: nevertheless I say unto you, HEREAFTER SHALL YE SEE THE SON OF MAN SITTING ON THE RIGHT HAND OF POWER, AND COMING IN THE CLOUDS OF HEAVEN.

Matthew 26:64

Ten Times Paul Had
Another World in View

The apostle Paul was a great example of sacrifice and fruitful ministry. He was relentless in his pursuit of souls. He gave up everything and went to the corners of the known world so that he could plant churches everywhere. Obviously, he had another world in view. This is the secret to the fruitfulness of the patriarchs of ministry: they had another world in view!

Although Paul had not ever lived in Heaven, his heart was fixed on the promised rewards of the other world. Unlike most other people, Paul did not seem to be afraid of death. Death and the after-world seemed to hold some kind of benefit for him. That is why he could make statements like, "To die is gain".

1. Therefore judge nothing before the time, until the Lord come, who both will bring to light the hidden things of darkness, and will make manifest the counsels of the hearts: and then shall every man have praise of God.

    1 Corinthian 4:5

2. For our light affliction, which is but for a moment, worketh for us a far more exceeding and eternal weight of glory; while we look not at the things which are seen, but at the things which are not seen: for the things which are seen are temporal; but the things which are not seen are eternal.

    2 Corinthians 4:17-18

3. For to me to live is Christ, and to die is gain.

    Philippians 1:21

4. For I am in a strait betwixt two, having a desire to depart, and to be with Christ; which is far better: nevertheless to abide in the flesh is more needful for you.

    Philippians 1:23-24

5.   I have fought a good fight, I have finished my course, I have kept the faith: henceforth there is laid up for me a crown of righteousness, which the Lord, the righteous judge, shall give me at that day: and not to me only, but unto all them also that love his appearing.

2 Timothy 4:7-8

6.   Know ye not that they which run in a race run all, but one receiveth the prize? So run, that ye may obtain. And every man that striveth for the mastery is temperate in all things. Now they do it to obtain a corruptible crown; but we an incorruptible.

1 Corinthians 9:24-25

7.   For we must all appear before the judgment seat of Christ; that every one may receive the things done in his body, according to that he hath done, whether it be good or bad.

2 Corinthians 5:10

8.   Therefore, my brethren dearly beloved and longed for, my joy and crown, so stand fast in the Lord, my dearly beloved.

Philippians 4:1

9.   For what is our hope, or joy, or crown of rejoicing? Are not even ye in the presence of our Lord Jesus Christ at his coming?

1 Thessalonians 2:19

10. And I knew such a man, (whether in the body, or out of the body, I cannot tell: God knoweth;) how that he was caught up into paradise, and heard unspeakable words, which it is not lawful for a man to utter. Of such an one will I glory: yet of myself I will not glory, but in mine infirmities.

2 Corinthians 12:3-5

CHAPTER 11

Barren Because You Are Short-Sighted

Our world has seven billion people today. If the statistics below remind you of the souls scattered all over the world, then you are not short-sighted.

If you are conscious of the statistics below, then you are not short-sighted.

When you are not short-sighted, you will be urged on by the realities the figures convey. You will no longer be deceived by the apparent success and achievements of the church today.

Can You See These Statistics?

a.   If the world had a 100 people, 60 of them would be from Asia.

b.   If the world had a 100 people, 13 of them would be from Africa.

c.   If the world had a 100 people, 12 of them would be from Europe.

d.   If the world had a 100 people, 9 of them would be from South America.

e.   If the world had a 100 people, 5 of them would be from North America.

f.   If the world had a 100 people, 1 would be from Oceania.

If you are short-sighted, you will never know these amazing statistics. The whole world is not made up of Americans. There is an impression that the world revolves in and around America. Is it not amazing that if the world had a hundred people sixty of them would actually come from Asia and only five from America? Is it not amazing that after Asia, Africa is the area of the world with the most number of people? In spite of these realities, most ministers swarm to the Americas to preach to the community already "saturated" with the Gospel.

Why Many Christians Are Fruitless

For if these things be in you, and abound, they make you that ye shall neither be barren nor unfruitful in the knowledge of our Lord Jesus Christ. But he that lacketh these things is blind, and CANNOT SEE AFAR off, and hath forgotten that he was purged from his old sins.

2 Peter 1:8-9

Short-Sightedness

Perhaps the greatest cause of barrenness in the church today is short-sightedness. The inability to see beyond our little community causes much of the barrenness of today's church. Our eyesight does not extend to the forgotten ones, the poor ones and the hungry souls that wait for our ministries to come to them. We only see the wealthy cities of this world. We only see the megachurches that make the offer of success and wealth to prosperity-seeking masses. These sights feed the deception that the whole world has been reached for Christ.

Jesus Christ Was Not Short-Sighted

Jesus lived and operated within a two-hundred mile radius. He never drove in a car or flew in a plane to other parts of the world. That did not make Him short-sighted. He saw way beyond Jerusalem. When He commissioned His disciples, He told them of Judea, Samaria and the uttermost parts of the world. He sent them to distant lands. He told them not to confine themselves to the small world of Jerusalem. There are others waiting and hoping that salvation would come to them too. The voice of Jesus is still ringing today, sending us to the uttermost parts of the world.

CHAPTER 12

Barren Because You Have Forgotten

For if these things be in you, and abound, they make you that ye shall neither be barren nor unfruitful in the knowledge of our Lord Jesus Christ. But he that lacketh these things is blind, and cannot see afar off, and HATH FORGOTTEN that he was purged from his old sins.

2 Peter 1:8-9

Why Many Christians Are Fruitless

Forgetfulness

Most of the church has forgotten how it came into existence. There is no church expansion without sacrifice. Almost every church and ministry came into existence through the blood and sacrifice of somebody. People are only saved when other Christians take up their crosses and follow Jesus. We have forgotten how salvation came to the peoples of this world. We will have to do what others did for them to be saved. We will have to give up our lives for the cause of the Gospel.

Missionaries travelled to Ghana, Nigeria, Malaysia, China and India giving up their lives for the cause of Jesus Christ. That is why there are Christians in these countries today. Much blood has been shed for the advancement of the message of Jesus Christ.

Hudson Taylor, the famous missionary to China, spent sixty years in China so that the Chinese people would know about Jesus Christ. He lost four wives and six children on the mission field! That is a lot of precious missionary blood to shed! Those are a lot of loved ones for one person to bury! That is a mighty high price for the Gospel of Jesus Christ to be preached.

But there is still a call for missionaries to be sent out. There is still a call for lives to be offered up. There is still a call for people to die serving the Lord! If you think that the day of dying for God and dying in His service is past, then you are deceived with a mighty delusion.

Do not forget this basic Christian principle: The cross of Jesus Christ and the sacrifice of our lives are the only ways for the true advancement of the church.

The prosperity, success, safety and security gospel will never save the world! It is the same message that is preached by banks and insurance companies. It is not the Gospel of Jesus Christ and will never be.

The Gospel of Jesus Christ is to *die* and to lose and *to give up* so that the Kingdom of God can advance. "Then said Jesus unto his disciples, If any man will come after me, let him deny himself, and take up his cross, and follow me. For whosoever will save his life shall lose it: and whosoever will lose his life for my sake shall find it" (Matthew 16:24-25).

Jesus Christ Was Not Forgetful

Even though most of us forget the basic truth of the cross, Christ never did. He never lost sight of His mission to lay down His life for the world. The crowds, the successful ministry and the miracles did not obscure the fact that He needed to shed His blood on the cross for mankind. He stopped His ministry of preaching and teaching and marched valiantly to Jerusalem where He knew He would be crucified.

On two different occasions, Peter tried to stop Jesus from going to the cross. He did this because he did not remember nor understand how salvation came through the blood sacrifice. On one occasion, Jesus called Peter the devil for trying to prevent Him going to the cross. "From that time forth began Jesus to shew unto his disciples, how that he must go unto Jerusalem, and suffer many things of the elders and chief priests and scribes, and be killed, and be raised again the third day. Then Peter took him, and began to rebuke him, saying, Be it far from thee, Lord: this shall not be unto thee. But he turned, and said unto Peter, Get thee behind me, Satan: thou art an offence unto me: for thou savourest not the things that be of God, but those that be of men" (Matthew 16:21-23).

On the second occasion, Peter actually took a sword to prevent the cross experience from coming on. This is exactly what Christians are doing today as they indirectly oppose and prevent young people from giving their lives for the work of God.

But Jesus had only one question to ask Peter: "SHALL I NOT DRINK THE CUP THAT MY FATHER HAS GIVEN ME TO DRINK? "Then Simon Peter having a sword drew it, and smote the high priest's servant, and cut off his right ear. The servant's name was Malchus. Then said Jesus unto Peter, Put up thy sword into the sheath: the cup which my Father hath given me, shall I not drink it? Then the band and the captain and officers of the Jews took Jesus, and bound him" (John 18:10-12).

CHAPTER 13

Obstacles to Bearing Fruit

1. You must overcome spiritual sicknesses in order to bear fruit.

The reason why some Christians do not bear fruit is because they are not healthy. They are not normal, productive Christians, because there is a *spiritual sickness* somewhere.

Sometimes when a woman is unable to give birth, it is due to an illness. Some causes of infertility are the blocking of the fallopian tubes, the inability of the ovaries to release eggs, the destruction of the womb due to an earlier abortion and so on. All these are *health* reasons, which prevent childbirth.

In the same way, when Christians are unable to give birth and be fruitful, it is often because there is some disease in their Christian life. Though they are born again, they are spiritually sick. One such sickness is laziness (some people are simply too lazy to labour for the Lord)! Another is pride. Also, many Christians are not productive because they are living in sin. Indeed, nothing affects fruitful Christian-living like sin does.

Some people have such bad, un-Christian habits that they cannot even muster the courage to share the Gospel. It is all a question of character.

I remember a certain Charismatic Christian who smoked so much that it became a problem in his office. Everybody complained about it, including his boss. Now, if somebody like this tried to preach to others, nobody would take him seriously. He probably would not even try, anyway! Such people are spiritually sick; that is why they cannot bring forth any fruit. But the Bible instructs us in 2 Peter 1:5-8 to add to our faith, virtue... temperance... patience... godliness... brotherly... kindness... charity. For if these things be in you, and abound, THEY MAKE YOU THAT YE SHALL NEITHER BE BARREN NOR UNFRUITFUL.

If these things be in you...they make you fruitful! Notice here that Peter lists a number of qualities which prevent us from becoming barren and unfruitful in the things of God. This is why some Christians are unfruitful; because they do not have virtue, temperance or brotherly kindness. The cancer of sin has made them unhealthy Christians. Unhealthy people everywhere are not productive.

2. **You must overcome the cares of the world in order to bear fruit.**

   And the cares of this world, and the deceitfulness of riches, and the lusts of other things entering in, choke the word, and it becometh unfruitful.

   Mark 4:19

   When the Word of God is choked, it means that its effect is blocked or obstructed. That is exactly what happens to some Christians. They become so occupied with other things that they no longer have time for the things of God.

   Read the text again, and notice that even the normal, everyday cares of life can retard your spiritual progress. The demands of your job, for example, the pressures of academic work or the challenges of bringing up little children can make you unfruitful.

Many Christians allow the blessings of marriage to choke the Word, and they end up no longer being useful to God. Some people behave as though their pregnancy was a disease. But I can tell you that it is not. They use pregnancy as an excuse to stop working for the Lord. In fact, some Christians are so mindful of the cares of this world, that all they have to offer are excuses:

"But Pastor, my children...my school...my business..."

What about the Lord's work? If you are too busy to be involved in winning souls, then you are *too busy*!

3. You must overcome the lusts and pleasures of this life in order to bear fruit.

The lust for many things is another killer and choker of the Word of God. Because of the desire to be someone important, people forsake the call of God. Because of the desire to live in certain countries, some reject the opportunity to be fruitful in the house of the Lord. Strong desires for things in this life can quench the call of God.

4. You must overcome the deceitfulness of riches in order to bear fruit.

God's blessings in our lives were not intended to keep us from doing His work. We must rather overcome these potential "chokers" and continue being fruitful in His vineyard. I look forward to the day when a judge would continue to play the drums in church. I look forward to the day when women will continue as pastors, in spite of the fact that they have four children. I look forward to the day when multimillionaires will continue to be ushers in church.

5. You must overcome distractions in order to bear fruit.

And he said unto them, GO YE INTO ALL THE WORLD, AND PREACH the gospel to every creature.

Mark 16:15

When I was in school, I was despised by some of my mates because I never participated much in athletics. I chose rather to concentrate on my studies (after all, that was why I was there). Looking at the way some people trained for athletic events, you would think that was the main reason why they were in school.

When the final exam results came in, I had a distinction, while some of my popular athletic colleagues "bombed" miserably. You see, they missed the point. Instead of concentrating on the primary goal of graduating with good grades, they were distracted from their studies by sports. They were mistaken because they did not set their priorities right.

As Christians, we must be steadfast and unmoved, no matter what is happening around us. We must have a vision because without a vision, we will be distracted from our purpose. Even as a pastor, I do not preoccupy myself with too many "political" meetings (we are talking about inter-church politics here.) I actually determine to stay away from such meetings. This is because I want to remain focused on the vision of winning souls.

The Church of God is the only institution in this world charged with preaching the Gospel, casting out devils, and upholding the truth of God's Word. We should therefore not deviate into party politics, inter-church politics, trading, or secular education.

Therefore, my beloved brethren, be ye steadfast, unmoveable, always [not sometimes] abounding in the work of the Lord...
1 Corinthians 15:58

Here God is telling us as individuals, students, workers, and as a church, to *remain committed* to our objectives.

Have you noticed that rich, successful companies stay focused on their main objective? Take a successful company like Unilever, a prominent international manufacturing company. For generations, they have been making money in Ghana, regardless of the government in place. Governments have come and gone, but they have remained steadfast in their core business.

Christians must learn to carry on with their core business and not be distracted.

Multitudes are perishing, and there is much work to be done. Sadly, our attention is often diverted into insignificant things. There are bound to be a whole lot of things which can distract you. But the important thing is to win souls and make disciples for Jesus.

If only we can be steadfast and unmovable by keeping our focus on the Great Commission, we will not fail to bear fruit.

6. You must overcome immaturity in order to bear fruit.

Another reason why people do not bear fruit is because they are not mature in the things of God. A Christian without converts is immature. When you are not fully developed, you cannot have children. For instance, a girl who is five years old cannot give birth. This is because she is not yet mature or full-grown. After you are born again, your main aim must be to grow.

You must move from childhood to adulthood and from immaturity to maturity.

But there are a whole lot of Christians who remain in the infant stage. By the time they ought to have grown to the point where they also teach others, they still have need for somebody to follow them up. To them, the church service is like some drama on TV. All they remember about the sermon are the jokes.

An immature Christian runs around from church to church and from one programme to another looking for excitement.

If a famous prophet were to start a church across the street, they would immediately drop everything and go there!

Listen, are you looking for something new? Then let me tell you, there is nothing new under the sun. Do not be an airy Christian, blown about by every wind of doctrine.

Don't be shallow and childish, tossed to and fro with every wind. Become a stable Christian who knows what he is about, and does not allow anything to sway him.

The mature tree says, "I will not be moved. I will remain planted here, and focus on growing, till I bear my fruits."

Church of God, it is time to grow up! It is time to show by our fruits, that we are mature.

> **When I was a child, I spake...I understood...I thought as a child: but when I became a man, I put away childish things.**
>
> **1 Corinthians 13:11**

7. **You must overcome the tendency to be unstable, in order to bear fruit.**

> **...the branch cannot bear fruit of itself, except it abide...He that abideth in me and I in him, the same bringeth forth much fruit...**
>
> **John 15:4, 5**

Jesus is saying here that you and I cannot bear fruit, except we abide in Him. This means to stay, or be planted; to be resident; to remain in Christ; to continue in the things of God.

You see, you have to abide in the same place for some time in order to become productive in that very place.

After all, every tree has to be nurtured over a period of time until it can bear fruits on its own. No mango tree can bear fruits after just one year. It will take several years of being planted in one place, to bear fruit.

For example, many of the pastors and elders in our church have been abiding here for a long time. They are abiding Christians who have developed into fruitful leaders. It is only by staying long enough to be watered and tended, that you can grow to become useful.

A lot of Christians do not allow themselves to get to the point of fruitfulness. Soon after they are planted, they uproot themselves. Today they are members here, tomorrow, they belong elsewhere. One day they are involved in this, the next time it is something else.

A tree that is often transplanted will never, ever grow to its full, fruit-bearing potential.

Older people are usually more stable in what they are doing. They seem to have a certain "staying anointing". Have you noticed that the members of the older Christian denominations will seldom, if ever, switch to another denomination?

Dear Christian, God wants you to have a restful spirit. Be stable in church. Be permanent. Abide. Make a quality decision to be planted in a Spirit-filled, Bible-believing church. Then decide to remain rooted until your fruits begin to show.

> **Those that be planted in the house of the LORD... shall still bring forth fruit in old age...**
> **Psalm 92:13, 14**

8. You must overcome inactivity in order to bear fruit.

Gynaecologists know for a fact that many childless couples are not sexually active. They just lie by each other like logs in a truck!

Some married women actually want children, but do not want to have sex. They "commit" love only about once a month, and then turn around to complain that they cannot have children.

That is how it is with some people. They are Christians alright, but because they are not active, they have no children— no converts, no fruits. Just look around, and you will observe that passive Christians bear no fruits.

Do you want to be pregnant and have children? Then you must engage in the activity that will make you pregnant. Do you want to be a fruitful Christian? Then you must engage in the activity that will make you fruitful. Witnessing, teaching, and helping in the church will all help you get active in the things of God!

Some people say, "But Pastor, I'm the quiet type, I don't want any trouble. I just prefer to mind my own business."

"I don't want to preach to my business partner, he'll think I'm odd."

And with such excuses we remain totally idle in a vineyard that is ripe for the harvest.

So how can we switch from being mere spectators to active participants?

...break up your fallow ground...

Hosea 10:12

Fallow ground is that which has been left dormant, idle, untouched and unused. And here the Lord is telling us to break up (cultivate) our fallow ground. That is, to utilize our untapped potential. Today there are a lot of genuine, but dormant Christians in the Church. They are gifted but do not use their gifts much.

Most people just sit there, doing nothing, while a few labourers do their best to fulfil the Great Commission. Because of this, it looks as if only a few are called, but the Word of God says that many are called. Many men! Many women! Many young people!

As you begin to use your talents and gifts in the service of the Lord, you will find yourself becoming more and more fruitful. Your regular Christian activity will yield results, and your fruits will definitely begin to show.

CHAPTER 14

Four Benefits of Bearing Fruit

1. Bearing fruit proves that you are a real Christian.

I have come to realize that all church members are not necessarily Christians. It is unfortunate, but many who go to church are not born again, and do not even know God.

Some years ago, we had a patient in the gynaecology department of the Korle-Bu Hospital, where I was working. This woman was in her early twenties, but had never been able to have her menstrual period. Now, as a doctor I knew that this was abnormal. When she was medically investigated and examined, we discovered that this "woman" was really a "man"! We found that she had hidden male reproductive organs. This explained why "she" was unable to have her menstrual period.

So in spite of what "she" looked like on the outside, "she" could never bear children because "she" was not a woman – "she" was a man. "She" was not real—"she" was a "he"!

That is why some people cannot bear fruit—because they are not real Christians. They are not genuine. They are like some shops in town, which are supposed to be boutiques and spare parts shops. Yet they never seem to be open for business. Every day they claim to be "taking stock", but in actual fact, they are doing some other illegal business behind the counter. Some people are simply not what they claim to be.

So, how can we tell whether you are a real Christian or not? Well, that is very simple:

Wherefore by their fruits ye shall know them.
Matthew 7:20

We can distinguish genuine Christians from counterfeit Christians by looking at their fruits! If, by your spiritual activity, others just like you are brought to the Lord and discipled, then this fruit you are bearing shows that you are real!

But if you have no converts to show for your Christianity, then there must be something missing. Perhaps you are not genuine. Perhaps you are just an attendee. No wonder some so-called Christians are not interested in the Bible or the things of God. (Their only response to the pastor's sermon is a big yawn!)

Today, many people come to church for reasons other than a deep desire to seek God. Others just follow a family member or a friend to church. That is why some people fall away when certain things happen – because they are not really what they claim to be.

For this reason, I keep telling the youth in our church, "If anyone wants to marry you, look at their fruits, and not at their pretty faces. By their fruits ye shall know them."

In a large church like ours, there are all sorts of beasts mingling with God's genuine flock. Wolves in sheep's clothing cannot bear witness for Christ. If something good has really happened to you, you will go about joyfully telling others. No one will have to urge you on. It just happens naturally.

Dear friend, if all your Christianity is going to church on Sundays, then you are missing a great deal of spiritual activity. Real Christianity takes place OUTSIDE the church AFTER Sundays. Each weekday must have its share of prayer, worship, Bible reading and labouring for the Lord.

So if you have always comforted yourself with the fact that you go to church on Sundays, then I am afraid I must "discomfort" you! Church membership does not prove you are a genuine Christian at all! Here is some sound advice from 2 Corinthians 13:5: "Examine yourselves, whether ye be in the faith."

Friend, be real. First, be born again. Then show by your fruit that you are a real, committed Christian.

2. Bearing fruit preserves your own kind in the church.

In the seventh chapter of Genesis, God commanded Noah to enter the ark with his wife, his three sons, and their wives.

In addition he was to take with him, male and female counterparts of every kind. Why was God so interested in preserving a sample of every kind of animal in the ark? It was to keep life going on the earth after the flood. Take a look at this verse:

> **Of fowls also of the air by seven, the male and the female; TO KEEP SEED ALIVE upon the face of the earth.**
>
> **Genesis 7:3**

The Helen Spurrel Translation of The Old Testament puts it this way:

> **...to preserve the species...**
>
> **Genesis 7:3**

By so doing, God has ensured the survival of each type of animal to this day, because He knew that Noah could never give birth to any of the other animals. He could only reproduce his own kind—human beings.

This same principle applies spiritually. Bearing fruit after your own kind will ensure that your particular "species" continues to exist in the church. You see, because I am bearing fruit after my own kind, there are many doctors in our church. There are several doctor-pastors in the ministry with me now. Some of them are even in full-time ministry.

I have preserved my own kind!

Now YOU too can begin to make converts of people who are just like you. This is your contribution to the growth and continuity of the church. Dear friend, just think about the increase we would have, if only the church of God would apply God's prescribed method–Individual Christians bearing fruit after their own kind.

As we all begin to operate in this way, we will surely experience a higher success rate in our personal evangelism, resulting in growth on all sides for the Body of Christ.

3. Bearing fruit will bring you much joy.

Lo, children are an heritage of the LORD...Happy is the man that hath his quiver full of them...

Psalm 127:3, 5

Here we understand that he who has many children is a happy man. However, children do not come so easily. In fact, when you consider the many painful and embarrassing things that happen at the labour ward, it makes you wonder, "Why do women want to have more children?"

First of all, there is the shame of exposing themselves to total strangers. Then there is the agony of labour itself. The pelvic bones actually move to allow the baby to come out. Sometimes when it becomes necessary to cut the women, their screams confirm the terrible pain they suffer. Really, it is not a small matter. (When I first observed a delivery, I had a renewed respect for women.)

So why do they do it over and over again? Jesus explained:

...she remembereth no more the anguish, for JOY that a man is born into the world.

John 16:21

After the baby is born, there's a joy that women feel, which I cannot possibly explain. Only those who have experienced it can explain it to you, but there's a supreme joy after childbirth. A deep fulfilment after having brought forth someone they can call their very own. It is this joy that makes them go through it again and again.

In the same way, there is a joy you will never experience till you lead others to be born again into the kingdom of God. For someone to be born again and stabilized in Christ under my ministry is a joy I cannot adequately express. The Bible says, "Happy is the man who has his quiver full of such children."

This is what keeps me going in the ministry, in spite of all the situations I face as a minister. Apart from often being away from my family, I have to endure a lot of ridicule and suspicion. Sometimes people treat you *despitefully*, because they assume you have nothing better to do.

I endure the shame, because of the unspeakable joy of winning souls for the Lord! You will never know this joy until YOU begin to bear fruit and see it growing.

4. **Bearing fruit will cause you not to be ashamed in the day of judgement.**

One of the most common verses engraved on many tombstones in our cemeteries is taken from Revelation 14:13. "...Blessed are the dead which die in the Lord from henceforth...that they may rest from their labours..."

Now notice: It did not say, "Blessed are those in the choir," or "Blessed are they that die in the church." Friends, it is a matter of being *in the Lord*, not just in the church!

But the text ends with a very important revelation: "...and their works do follow them."

When you die, you cannot take anything along with you. No, not your car, your money, or even your clothes. After death the only thing which can follow you are your works. That is, the fruit you have borne in your Christian life. The disciples you have established in the Lord are your Christian children. Now, concerning spiritual children, we learn that:

Happy is the man that hath his quiver full of them *[children]*: **they shall not be ashamed...**

Psalm 127:5

Very soon, you are going to stand before the judgement seat of Christ. Are you going to stand there empty-handed and ashamed? Or, will you bear your fruits now, so that your works can follow you?

CHAPTER 15

Ten Reasons Why People Do Not Use Their Talents

For the kingdom of heaven is as a man travelling into a far country, who called his own servants, and delivered unto them his goods. And unto one he gave five talents, to another two, and to another one; to every man according to his several ability; and straightway took his journey.

Then he that had received the five talents went and traded with the same, and made them other five talents. And likewise he that had received two, he also gained other two.

But he that had received one went and digged in the earth, and hid his lord's money. After a long time the lord of those servants cometh, and reckoneth with them.

Matthew 25:14-19

God has given everyone something to do. He has given
everybody a calling or a talent. This classic story by our
Lord Jesus illustrates this timeless truth to the Christian world.
Some people were given more talents than others but everybody
had something. Amazingly, some people did not use their gifts
and were not quiet about it either. They had a lot to say to the
master on the day of reckoning.

I believe that this story is one of the most vivid illustrations
of how God endows everyone with gifts and callings. Yet many
do not do anything at all with their gifts. In this section, I want
to share with you ten reasons why, I believe, many people do not
use their talents in spite of their calling. Some people simply do
nothing with their talents and their gifts.

1. FIRST REASON: FEAR

**And I WAS AFRAID, and went and hid thy talent in
the earth...**

Matthew 25:25

Fear is an evil spirit which paralyses Christians into inactivity.
Perhaps, it is one of the greatest forces that keep people from
taking up their talents and using them. At many junctions of
my life, fear attempted to paralyze me into inactivity and
fruitlessness. I can remember several times when fear tried to
keep me from serving God and using my talents.

1. The fear of starting a church

When I was going to start the church, I was full of fear that
it may not work. My assistant pastor discussed with me about
starting the church outside the city of Accra in a town called
Nsawam.

He suggested, "Why don't we start this church in Nsawam so
that if it doesn't work, no one will know." I tell you, it was a very
appealing suggestion because there were fears raging in my heart
about whether the church would work or not. Nevertheless, I put

aside my fears and went ahead and started a church, from scratch. Today, that church has grown and become a blessing to many.

2.   The fear of full-time ministry

Going into full-time ministry was another fearful proposition for me.

"How would I survive? How would I live? How would my children be able to go to school? What about if it didn't work? Was I going to make a fool of myself and my family by leaving medicine and going into full-time ministry work? How would I feel if people laughed at me because of my poverty and beggarly life?"

These were real fears that attempted to keep me from using my talents. But, I put them aside and pressed on. I have learnt that fear is a powerful force that can keep you from fulfilling the call of God.

3.   The fear of praying for the sick in my church

When I felt the Lord leading me to pray for the sick, I was, once again, gripped with many fears. You see, fear is a spirit that keeps you from using your talents, gifts and callings. I had never experienced fear and tension as I did when I launched out to begin praying for the sick and receiving testimonies. I feared that no one would be healed and that I would be embarrassed beyond imagination.

Somehow, I overcame those fears, went ahead and began miracle services where I boldly asked people to testify of their healings. This was the beginning of miracles and my greatest barrier to this ministry was fear.

4.   The fear of praying for the sick outside my church

I can never forget the first time I prayed for the sick outside my church. I was terrified beyond imagination. I prayed and fasted all day until the programme in the evening. Throughout my sermon, I could think of only one thing: "Will you or will you not pray for the sick when you finish preaching?"

"Don't bother to pray for the sick," the devil said to me. "It will not work and you will only disgrace yourself."

Satan persisted, "Praying for the sick in this church will yield no results because you have not hypnotized them as you have done in your church."

He continued, "These people will not accept psychological changes as healings."

It was one of the greatest battles of my life to overcome those fears. Indeed, to simply pray for the sick and ask for testimonies in someone else's church had become a great battle. Somehow, I managed to overcome those fears and there were powerful testimonies that night. There was no one as happy as myself to have gotten over the ordeal of that night's service.

5.   The fear of praying for the sick in another country

Yet another challenge awaited me. One day, I received an invitation to come preach in South Africa. I had successfully prayed for the sick and called for testimonies in my church and outside my church, but I had never done it outside Ghana.

The devil said to me, "Do not attempt any of these psychological healing services in South Africa. It will not work outside Ghana. Ghanaians are fickle and will believe in your make-believe healing ministry. There is no need to embarrass yourself on the international scene."

Once again, I struggled to overcome my fears of praying for the sick. And yet, praying for the sick became one of the most important things I did on that trip. I overcame my fears and used the talent that God had given me. By overcoming these fears, I entered a much higher realm of ministry.

6.   The fear of publishing books

One day, the Lord asked me to write a book.

I thought to myself, "Who would read my books?"

I remember struggling through the first manuscripts and spacing out the sentences so that the book would become larger. Eventually, when the books were produced they looked so slim and childish that I was ashamed of them. I thought that no one would read what I had written. Indeed, I am surprised by the way the Lord has used my books.

It is very important to overcome your fears since they will keep you from using your talents or obeying the call from God.

7. The fear of having crusades

Some years ago, I felt the Lord leading me to hold gospel crusades. But I was plagued with the fear that no one would come to the crusade and I would fall flat on my face in disgrace.

"Who made you an evangelist? Who do you think you are?
No one knows you! You are not known as a healing evangelist!
You are just a teacher and a church administrator!
Why do you want to be disgraced at this stage of your ministry?"

These were just a few of the demonic and fearful thoughts that raged through my mind. I remember, as if it was yesterday, the first day I stood on a platform to preach at a crusade. I smiled to myself on stage as I looked at the sea of people in the large gospel tent.

"It's happening! The crusades have begun in spite of all the attempts to prevent them from coming on."

Do not allow fear to keep you from obeying the call. Fear is an evil spirit. Do not follow an evil spirit, follow the Holy Spirit.

2. SECOND REASON: HIDING YOUR GIFTS

AND I was afraid, and WENT AND HID thy talent in the earth...

Matthew 25:25

Fear causes you to hide your gifts. Many people conceal who they are and what they can do. No one knows their potential because it is well concealed. Have you hidden your talents and gifts? Perhaps fear of criticism has caused you to hide your gifts of singing, teaching, or even giving.

3. THIRD REASON: A FAULT-FINDING ATTITUDE

Then he which had received the one talent came and said, LORD, I KNEW THEE THAT THOU ART AN HARD MAN, reaping where thou hast not sown, and gathering where thou hast not strawed:

Matthew 25:24

The gentleman with one talent did nothing because he found fault with the master who sent him forth. He described him as a *hard man* who *benefited* from things *he did not deserve.*

Fault-finding is a common characteristic of fruitless and inactive people! Instead of getting involved in the work of God, they sit back and analyze others who are fighting hard to do something for God. It is not difficult to find fault with someone or something if you are looking for it. And what will you find about people who are striving to serve the Lord? Faults! Faults! Faults!

But the faults you find will only become the reason for you to withhold your own abilities. Why even bother to look for faults in God's servant? God did not choose angels to work for Him. He chose flaw-ridden men and women of varying backgrounds to do His work. You will always find something wrong when you look closely at God's servants.

People even lose their chance to be saved because they find fault with Christians!

Have you ever heard someone say, "I don't want to be a Christian because all those Christians are hypocrites"?

Have you ever heard someone say, "Those preachers are just looking for money"?

People miss the grace and the gift of God because they find fault with pastors. Put away fault-finding and you will become fruitful.

Stop focusing on the faults of others and focus on what you can do for God. Can you imagine if someone decided to focus on your inadequacies and shortcomings? You would not stand a chance! This story teaches us that those who focused on the faults of the leader did nothing, but those who focused on the task before them became fruitful.

4. FOURTH REASON: DESPISING THE TYPE OF GIFT YOU HAVE

Then he which had received THE ONE TALENT came and said, Lord, I knew thee that thou art an hard man, reaping where thou hast not sown, and gathering where thou hast not strawed:

Matthew 25:24

The gentleman who received one talent did not use his talent. He assumed that this talent would not yield much. In other words, he despised what he had been given. Many people feel they cannot preach as well as some of the well-known preachers of the world. Perhaps you know that you could never have a really large church. Perhaps, you feel you have just been given some *bland, featureless gift*. You complain because there is nothing remarkable about your gift. For this reason, you simply tuck it out of sight.

Years ago, I listened to a preacher describe his dramatic salvation experience. He told of how he burnt his fingers in fire under the instructions of evil spirits. He would lift up his fingers and show us how they were cut off. Then he would launch into various exciting tales of his past worldly life. This preacher would urge the crowds to come to Christ with his motivating and exciting testimony. I cannot help but remember how I thought I would never be able to evangelise people like he did. I simply did not have all these fantastic stories to tell. I knew I had received a more *ordinary gift.* I was like the fellow with one talent. It was up to me to despise my ordinary gift or use it as it was. And I did use it! Do not despise your one talent. It is good enough to do the job.

5. FIFTH REASON: DESPISING THE SMALLNESS OF YOUR GIFT

And I was afraid, and went and HID THY TALENT IN THE EARTH: lo, there thou hast that is thine.

Matthew 25:25

Perhaps, the man who received one talent thought it was too small to make any significant profit. He felt it was better to do nothing than to waste his time working with only one talent. Despising your calling because of its apparent smallness is one of the most dangerous spiritual mistakes you could ever make.

In our world, anything that is small is despised. A small house, a small car, a small town, a small man, a small woman are all mentally stereotyped as being insignificant. This is not so in the kingdom of God. Jesus taught us to respect small things. He taught us that the kingdom of God is like a tiny mustard seed but will grow to become a powerful and significant force in spite of its small start in size.

Twenty years ago, if I had despised the small fellowship of students I called a church, I would have no ministry today. I did not despise the smallness of my early ministry. God has shown me that small things in the kingdom are truly significant.

6. SIXTH REASON: OVER-ESTIMATING YOUR ABILITIES

And unto one he gave five talents, to another two, and to another one; TO EVERY MAN ACCORDING TO

HIS SEVERAL ABILITY; and straightway took his journey.

Matthew 25:15

Sometimes people might think of themselves as being above certain tasks. They feel demeaned by being asked to do certain jobs.

Perhaps you think that your gift is too small and that you deserve to do more in the house of the Lord. Do not forget the fact that Jesus gave talents according to abilities. You cannot do everything and you are not qualified or even able to do certain things. You must be content with what God has allowed you to do because He has given you gifts according to your ability.

7. SEVENTH REASON: LAZINESS

His lord answered and said unto him, Thou wicked and SLOTHFUL SERVANT, thou knewest that I reap where I sowed not, and gather where I have not strawed:

Matthew 25:26

Ministry involves hard work. You cannot do much for God if you are lazy. I have come to see that it is only hard-working people who accomplish much in the ministry. One of the commonest causes for fruitlessness is plain old laziness!

8. EIGHTH REASON: NOT WANTING TO BE CHEATED

His lord answered and said unto him, Thou wicked and slothful servant, thou knewest that I reap where I sowed not, and gather where I have not strawed:

Matthew 25:26

Let this mind be in you, which was also in Christ Jesus:Who, being in the form of God, THOUGHT IT NOT ROBBERY to be equal with God: But made

himself of no reputation, and took upon him the form of a servant, and was made in the likeness of men:

Philippians 2:5-7

Not wanting to be "cheated" is another important reason why people do nothing for God. The mind that, "I am being cheated" is a thought which paralyzes the average person into inaction. Many developing countries do not realise that this is the reason why they are unable to develop. The notion that rich people, or even rich countries, are cheating them prevents them from signing certain agreements that would benefit the whole country.

Just the thought that someone is cheating you will cause you to withdraw and hold back. No one likes to be cheated; that is why it is a successful strategy to let people feel that they are being cheated if you want them to be inactive. Many people do not work in their churches because they feel the pastor is cheating them. This causes many talents to remain hidden and unused.

There are those who say, "Why should I go to work and give ten per cent of what I earn to this lazy pastor?"

They say, "Why should he sleep at home all week and receive ten per cent of my income? That is cheating and I will not have any of it!"

As you can see, a feeling of "being cheated" makes people inactive.

9. NINTH REASON: WICKEDNESS

His lord answered and said unto him, Thou WICKED and slothful SERVANT, thou knewest that I reap where I sowed not, and gather where I have not strawed:

Matthew 25:26

One day, a fine gentleman was walking down the street on his way to work. He was on his way to the prestigious bank where he worked as one of the managers. He was known in town as a good moral Christian with a strong sense of righteous living.

This devout Christian man began his day in the office with a morning devotion. He was also known to be a man with strong family values who took his children to the local swimming club every week as he himself was a very good swimmer.

One day, on his way to work, he spotted a child shouting for help in the river which ran through his city. The person in the river was shouting, splashing and causing a big commotion as she tried to get the attention of passers-by. A little crowd of on-lookers had gathered on the shore hoping that someone who could swim would save the little girl.

This fine gentleman was, however, on his way to work and needed to be on time for his board meeting. He decided to ignore the screams for help and passed on. He arrived at his office on time to have the morning devotion with his staff.

Later that day, the body of the person who had screamed for help from the river was washed ashore and taken to the local mortuary. This nice Christian gentleman carried on with his life and became more and more acclaimed as a perfect example of good Christian character.

You could describe this man as "wicked" because he did not help to save the little child even though he could have. But why do you call him a wicked man? Did he hurt anyone? The answer is "No!" Did he kill anyone? The answer is "No!" Did he harm anyone? The answer is "No!" Then why do you call him a wicked man? BECAUSE HE DID NOTHING!

You see, dear friend, doing nothing can be wickedness! That is why Jesus called the man who did nothing with his talent a "wicked and unprofitable" servant. The words "wicked servant" have a profound meaning, deeper than we may care to meditate on. If you do nothing with the talent that God has given you, it may cause many people to go to Hell. And that is wickedness! Avoid being called a wicked servant by using your talents, your gifts and your calling.

10. TENTH REASON: BEING SPIRITUALLY UNPROFITABLE, WORTHLESS AND USELESS

Take therefore the talent from him, and give it unto him which hath ten talents. For unto every one that hath shall be given, and he shall have abundance: but from him that hath not shall be taken away even that which he hath. And cast ye the UNPROFITABLE SERVANT into outer darkness: there shall be weeping and gnashing of teeth.

Matthew 25:28-30

At the end of this parable, Jesus declared the servant to be unprofitable, worthless and useless. Sometimes, we make the mistake of acquiring something that is useless. I once acquired a pair of shoes that were too tight. When I got home and tried them on, I realised that I could not wear them. I could not also return them because I was no more in the country where I got them. This beautiful pair of shoes, although expensive, became absolutely useless and worthless to me.

Has God made a mistake of saving someone like you? After He has washed you with His precious blood and made you into a new creation, have you turned out to be an unprofitable servant?

Are you useless and worthless to God?

Are you of any use when it comes to saving people and doing the work of God? Please do not become one of the unprofitable and worthless Christians in your church.

CHAPTER 16

The Appointed Times of Your Spiritual Life

...a time to pluck up that which is planted...

Ecclesiastes 3:2

...time to heal...

Ecclesiastes 3:3

...a time to gather stones together...

Ecclesiastes 3:5

A time to get...

Ecclesiastes 3:6

...a time of war...

Ecclesiastes 3:8

There is no time in the spirit world. Time is a reality that has to do with this present earthly world. A time will come when this concept of time as we know it will not exist anymore. "And the angel which I saw stand upon the sea and upon the earth lifted up his hand to heaven, and sware by him that liveth for ever and ever, who created heaven, and the things that therein are, and the earth, and the things that therein are, and the sea, and the things which are therein, *that there should be time no longer*" (Revelation 10:5-6). You will notice, as you grow older, that you do not feel mentally or psychologically older. Actually, you tend to think and feel as though you were the same youthful age. It is only certain signs in your body that reveal that time is passing by.

You must understand the implications of earthly time as it relates to your life. This is especially important if you wish to work for God.

God has given us this time on earth as a gift of grace to prove our love for Him. Our time on earth is also a test which we must pass in order to obtain higher glories for eternity. We will forever look back to the period of time we were put on earth and given the opportunity to do something for Him.

Remember that we cannot come back. Remember that we cannot "do earth" again. This is it. It's once and for all and you must get it right the first time. Unfortunately, most people understand life when it is all over. But for wisdom to be useful, it must be applied when you are young. Wisdom is intended to help you to live a better life. Wisdom will not help you much at the end of your life. The purpose of wisdom is not to make you look back and regret your past life. The purpose of wisdom is to make you have a better life in the future. That is why wisdom must be applied in your youth.

In this chapter, I want to share a few things about time as it relates to your period on earth.

"And if ye call on the Father, who without respect of persons judgeth according to every man's work, pass the time of your sojourning here in fear" (1 Peter 1:17).

You are welcome to this earth! For your information, this is a world where time is both relevant and important. One of the things you will discover is the fact that there are appointed times for many things. There was a time for you to be born, and that is when you were born. There is a time for you to die, and that is when you will die.

> **For the days shall come upon thee, that thine enemies shall cast a trench about thee, and compass thee round, and keep thee in on every side,**
>
> **And shall lay thee even with the ground, and thy children within thee; and they shall not leave in thee one stone upon another; because thou knewest not the time of thy visitation.**
>
>

Luke 19:43-44

Notice ten important appointed times that will affect your work for God.

1. The time of your birth

> **A time to be born, and a time to die;**
>
>

Ecclesiastes 3:2

> **Is any thing too hard for the Lord? AT THE TIME APPOINTED I will return unto thee, according to the time of life, and Sarah shall have a son.**
>
>

Genesis 18:14

The importance of this time is that it is related to the lives of other people who will live around the same time that it has been appointed for you to live. Sometimes, the births of people are delayed in order to ensure that certain people live on the earth at the same time.

A good example of people who had to live on earth around the same time were Jesus Christ and John the Baptist. In fact, the birth of John the Baptist was delayed in order to ensure that he lived at the time to make the way for the Lord. This played out through the barrenness of Elizabeth who was divinely prevented from giving birth to John the Baptist until she was an old lady. From today, look out carefully for people whose birth and ages have been divinely timed with yours in order for you to meet them. Do not take these things for granted because a spiritual person believes in the power of God rather than in chance and happenstance.

Sometimes, even a gap of just ten years can make the difference between a person's relevance to you, your life and your ministry. I believe that many of the people that are with me today were born and guided divinely so that our lives would coincide and God's purpose be fulfilled. I do not take anyone for granted because different people play different life-changing roles at different times.

A time to be born, and a time to die...
Ecclesiastes 3:2

2.   The time of your death

For I am now ready to be offered, and THE TIME OF MY DEPARTURE is at hand.
2 Timothy 4:6

The time of your death is another appointment that is divinely determined. The importance of this time is that it reveals how many years were predetermined for your stay on earth. Everyone has a predetermined period granted to him on arrival to earth (Job 14:5). It is amazing that such concepts are difficult for Christians to fathom, when they are practised around us all the time.

When you enter a country, you are always given a fixed period to stay there. Sometimes, you are given a year; sometimes you are given six months. If more grace has been granted to you, you may even be given a five-year visa. Similarly, if a lot of grace has been given to you, you will live for a long time. Sometimes there are reasons for short stays and short lives that everyone can understand.

Sometimes, it is difficult to understand why some people live long and others much shorter. It is equally difficult to understand why some people are given longer visas and others, very short ones. This "long or short stay" is what determines how much time you have and what you can do.

It is because of the different times allotted to all of us that the concept of *my time* and *your time* comes into play. Jesus spoke of His time being different from the time of the apostles. "Then Jesus said unto them, MY TIME is not yet come: but YOUR TIME is alway ready. The world cannot hate you; but me it hateth, because I testify of it, that the works thereof are evil. Go ye up unto this feast: I go not up yet unto this feast; for MY TIME is not yet full come" (John 7:6-8).

This revelation is very important because it shows how we must all, individually, work for God irrespective of what the other person is doing. That person may have seventy years to live whilst you may have only thirty-nine. You may both be thirty-nine years old thinking that you have thirty-one more years to work for the Lord whereas you actually have just a few more months to go. Your friend next door, who is equally backslidden, may actually be given many more years to recover and do well in ministry because his time is different from your time.

Jesus Christ knew that His time was different from the apostles' time. He knew that they had more time than He did, so He said to them, "Your time is alway ready." Become conscious of the time that God has allotted to you. It is possible to know and sense the end of your time. Paul sensed he was near the time of his death and he said, "For I am now ready to be offered, and the time of my departure is at hand" (2 Timothy 4:6).

3. **The time of your salvation**

(For he saith, I have heard thee in a time accepted, and in the day of salvation have I succoured thee: behold, NOW IS THE ACCEPTED TIME; BEHOLD, NOW IS THE DAY OF SALVATION.)

2 Corinthians 6:2

The Scripture above cannot be clearer. There is a time to be saved. There is a day of salvation. There is an hour and a moment that God has destined an opportunity for your salvation.

God ignored the sins of people because it was not *the time* for repentance and salvation. "And the times of this ignorance God winked at; but now commandeth all men every where to repent: because he hath appointed a day, in the which he will judge the world in righteousness by that man whom he hath ordained; whereof he hath given assurance unto all men, in that he hath raised him from the dead" (Acts 17: 30-31).

However, when the time came for salvation, God required and expected men to repent and turn away from their sins. Failure to repent in the times of ignorance did not result in judgment. God simply winked at them. But failure to repent in the day of salvation will result in God's severe judgment.

The time of your salvation is the time allotted for you to be saved. You will notice that it becomes more difficult to be saved, as you get older. For many people God has assigned a time of salvation in their youth. When you pass the time of your salvation, it is almost impossible to be saved.

Let us recognize that God has appointed times for various important events of our lives. Why is it hard for us to believe this when every school has allotted time for lectures, exams, sports, vacation and other activities? Everyone, including parents, have to fit into these timetables. When the times of exams are passed, you cannot go back and sit for that particular exam anymore.

Understanding the reality that there is a time for salvation will guide ministers to emphasize a ministry to young people who may be at *the time* of their salvation.

4. The time for your maturity

For when for THE TIME YE OUGHT TO BE TEACHERS, ye have need that one teach you again which be the first principles of the oracles of God;

and are become such as have need of milk, and not of strong meat.

Hebrews 5:12

Every baby that is born into this world is expected to mature into certain things at particular times. Any variations from these set times cause much worry for both parents and doctors.

- By the time you are four weeks old, you are supposed to recognize your mother's voice.

- By the time you are six weeks, you are supposed to smile at your mother.

- By four months you are supposed to be able to roll over.

- By six months, you should be able to sit by yourself with minimal support.

- By seven month you should be crawling.

- By nine months, you should be able to stand with support.

- By twelve months you should be walking.

Similarly, God has certain fixed times that He expects certain things from every Christian. Things just do not happen haphazardly. There is a plan and there is a time for everything. After your salvation, there is a time set for your maturation. At the time of your maturation, you are expected to graduate from your interest in milk and milky products to meat. This simply means you develop a greater interest in deeper aspects of the Word of God. Part of this maturation process is your graduation from being a receiver only, to becoming someone who teaches the Word of God as well. Beginning to teach the Word of God from your heart is one of the greatest signs of your maturity.

Unfortunately, many Christians remain in churches for years and are unable to lead a simple Bible study. This is a sad reality. When Christians miss the time of their maturation, they often do not mature at a later date. They often develop features of spiritual imbeciles who speak with great swelling words of emptiness. They often manifest their emptiness by their foolish talk. An imbecile is someone who "has a mental age of three to seven years." You can imagine what it is like when a woman who has been in church for twenty-five years speaks about issues with the spiritual maturity of a three year old.

When people have been members of churches for many years and have not matured, they are also deluded into thinking they are something they are not. They equate their natural age with their spiritual age and you can only guess the confusion that arises in the church.

5. The time for your anointing

Does the rain fall all the time? Certainly not. There is a time for the rain to fall and similarly there is a time for the Holy Spirit to come upon your life.

Just as there is a time for you to receive salvation, God has also scheduled a time for you to receive the Holy Spirit and become anointed. The Holy Spirit does not haphazardly fall on people irrespective of the time. Notice in the Scripture below that the disciples were asked to wait for the promise of the Holy Spirit. The Holy Spirit fell on them at a particular time and they had to wait for it.

> **To whom also he shewed himself alive after his passion by many infallible proofs, being seen of them forty days, and speaking of the things pertaining to the kingdom of God:**
>
> **And, being assembled together with them, commanded them that they should not depart from Jerusalem, but WAIT FOR THE PROMISE of the Father, which, saith he, ye have heard of me.**
>
> **Acts 1:3-4**

The gift of the Holy Spirit is the most precious thing you could ever have from God. God wants to bless you but if you are not prepared to wait, you will not receive it. If you are not ready when it is time you will miss the pouring out of the Holy Spirit.

> **Repent ye therefore, and be converted, that your sins may be blotted out, WHEN THE TIMES OF**

REFRESHING SHALL COME from the presence of the Lord;

Acts 3:19

6. The time for your fruitfulness

And seeing a fig tree afar off having leaves, he came, if haply he might find any thing thereon: and when he came to it, HE FOUND NOTHING BUT LEAVES; for the time of figs was not yet. And Jesus answered and said unto it, No man eat fruit of thee hereafter for ever. And his disciples heard it.

Mark 11:13-14

And in the morning, as they passed by, they saw the fig tree dried up from the roots. And Peter calling to remembrance saith unto him, Master, behold, the fig tree which thou cursedst is withered away.

Mark 11:20-21

The story of Jesus cursing the fig tree is not readily understood by most Christians. Why should Jesus curse a tree which does not have fruits for Him to eat? Another question is, why did Jesus curse the tree knowing that it was not the season for figs? The answer to these questions is simple: There is a time that God expects fruit from you. If you do not have the fruits when He wants them you may receive a deathly curse. "For the earth which drinketh in the rain that cometh oft upon it, and bringeth forth herbs meet for them by whom it is dressed, receiveth blessing from God: But that which beareth thorns and briers is rejected, and is nigh unto cursing; whose end is to be burned" (Hebrews 6:7-8).

When God requires fruit from you, you better produce those fruits otherwise you could be subject to a curse. It is not about when you want to bear fruit. It is not about whether it is a convenient season for figs or not. It is not about when *you* are ready to work for God. It is not about when it is convenient for you to come into full-time ministry. The question to be asked is, "When does *God* want the fruit?"

If God wants fruit from you when you are twenty-five years old, you cannot put him off for forty years and tell Him to wait till you are sixty-five. Have you ever heard of a president offering a job to someone and being put off for ten years? Usually not. Most people would jump at every opportunity that comes from the president. How much more when Almighty God stretches out His hand of opportunity to give you a job in His vineyard. Who are you to turn away this invitation? Do not be surprised if you inherit a curse in your life because you do not bear fruit for the Lord *when* He expects you to bear those fruits.

I became a pastor when I was a medical student. All the fruits that I have borne and all the souls that have been won would have been lost if I had told the Lord that it was not the time of figs and that He should come at another season of my life.

7. The time for your special spiritual visitation

Abraham had very special visitations of angels. How blessed he was! I do envy him as I have not received such a visit in my life. But even Abraham had a time at which this visitation was to happen. Indeed, spiritual events occur with special timing so that you will accomplish particular things at a particular time.

> **Is any thing too hard for the LORD? At THE TIME APPOINTED I will return unto thee, according to the time of life, and Sarah shall have a son.**
> **Genesis 18:14**

There are ministers who have done everything right: they have prayed, they have fasted, they have listened to tapes and they have sought the Lord many times. They are seeking a special visitation from the Lord or a special anointing to do the works of God.

However, these great blessings do not just drop out of the heavens every evening. God has a time scheduled for special visitations. Jesus spoke of the time of visitation when Jerusalem was visited by the Son of God Himself.

And shall lay thee even with the ground, and thy children within thee; and they shall not leave in thee one stone upon another; because thou knewest not THE TIME OF THY VISITATION.

Luke 19:44

In 1988, God anointed me in a little town called Suhum, in Ghana. I had been a Christian for many years, but suddenly, and without announcement, I received a special anointing to teach the Word of the Lord. That was a special visitation.

Since then, I have been seeking other visitations of the Lord, including a visitation of the Lord Jesus Himself. I have longed for and prayed for angels to appear to me as well as to have wonderful visions of Heaven.

Unfortunately, as I write this book, I still have not received any of these visitations. If it is the Lord's will to grant me these special visitations, I know there will be a special time at which they will be granted.

This is why there are times when you have dreams and visions, while at other times you have no dreams and no visions for a long time. Sometimes, you just enter a season or a time where there will be no special visitation.

8.   The time for your enlargement

And another angel came out of the temple, crying with a loud voice to him that sat on the cloud, THRUST IN THY SICKLE, AND REAP: FOR THE TIME IS COME for thee to reap; for the harvest of the earth is ripe. And he that sat on the cloud thrust in his sickle on the earth; and the earth was reaped.

Revelation 14:15-16

There is a time that God grants enlargement and expansion. In the Scripture above, the angel declared in the heavenly realms that the time had come to reap a great harvest in the earth. This was not just any ordinary harvest but a time of great productivity and fruitfulness. If you study the lives of ministers, you will notice a particular time at which they become greatly enlarged and extremely well known.

This is a kind of enlargement and visibility that God grants to His servants at a time He has already determined. This enlargement enables the minister to reap a mighty harvest for the Lord. Usually, there is much preparation and suffering before this season of enlargement. This season of preparation is to humble His servant so that he can carry the awesome responsibility of an enlarged and visible ministry.

There was a time when Jesus' brothers urged Him to prematurely enter His season of enlargement and high public visibility. Jesus knew all about the implications of such a high profile and visible ministry. He declined because it was not yet time for such things.

> **His brethren therefore said unto him, Depart hence, and go into Judaea, that thy disciples also may see the works that thou doest.**
> **For there is no man that doeth any thing in secret, and he himself seeketh to be known openly. If thou do these things, shew thyself to the world...Then Jesus said unto them, My time is not yet come: but your time is alway ready.**
>
> **John 7:3-4, 6**

You will notice that within a week of Jesus' accepting the large, public and visible ministry, by marching into Jerusalem on a donkey with thousands of adoring followers, He was brutally murdered on a Roman cross by jealous and insecure Jewish ministers.

Enlarged public ministry can be likened to when a snake comes out into the open. It is not long before people to decide to eliminate that snake.

9. The time of your testing

Wherefore take unto you the whole armour of God, that ye may be able to withstand in THE EVIL DAY, and having done all, to stand.

Ephesians 6:13

There is also the time appointed in your life to experience evil and overcome it. This is what is called the evil day. It is a day to expect and a day which comes to Christians no matter their beliefs. Days of evil and days of testing also have seasons and special times of appearance. "Those by the way side are they that hear; then cometh the devil, and taketh away the word out of their hearts, lest they should believe and be saved. They on the rock are they, which, when they hear, receive the word with joy; and these have no root, which for a while believe, and IN TIME OF TEMPTATION fall away" (Luke 8:12-13).

Part of your spiritual accomplishments is to overcome the evil and the temptations that will befall you as you serve the Lord.

Be not overcome of evil, but overcome evil with good.

Romans 12:21

10. The time for your judgement

Heaven and earth shall pass away: but my words shall not pass away. But of that day and that hour knoweth no man, no, not the angels which are in heaven, neither the Son, but the Father. Take ye heed, watch and pray: for ye know not when THE TIME is.

Mark 13:31-33

Judgement waits for all of us but no one knows when it will come. It is yet another appointment that we cannot avoid no matter our beliefs and opinions. We must die and give account to the Lord for our wretched lives. "And as it is appointed unto men once to die, but after this the judgment" (Hebrews 9:27).

On the Day of Judgement, we will account for what we did for the Lord when He gave us the chance to work for Him. "For we must all appear before the judgment seat of Christ; that every one may receive the things done in his body, according to that he hath done, whether it be good or bad" (2 Corinthians 5:10). It is not enough to be born again. You must also work for God because you will account for the life you lived in your earthly body.

This judgement is something we must look forward to and live in such a way that that day will not be a day of grief and regret. Obey them that have the rule over you, and submit yourselves: for they watch for your souls, as they that must give account, that they may do it with joy, and not with grief: for that is unprofitable for you" (Hebrews 13:17).

Another reality about judgement is that some people start paying for their sins earlier than others. Some people commit sin and seem to get away with it. God has a particular time of judgement for everyone. You may commit crimes with someone who has judgement day set for somewhere in the future whilst your judgement day is set for much sooner. It is these differences in judgement dates that make it seem as though some people get away with sin whilst others seem to suffer so much after one little crime. All this goes to emphasize the truth that every one of us has a different timetable for different events that God has predetermined.

Some men's sins are open beforehand, going before to judgment; and some men they follow after. Likewise also the good works of some are manifest beforehand; and they that are otherwise cannot be hid.

1 Timothy 5:24-25

CHAPTER 17

Redeeming the Time

See then that ye walk circumspectly, not as fools, but as wise, REDEEMING THE TIME, because the days are evil.

Ephesians 5:15-16

To redeem the time is to use your little opportunity on this earth as much as possible. Your time is a precious commodity given as a gift to you. Your years on this earth are the blessed opportunity given to prove your love for the Lord.

LORD, make me to know my end And what is the extent of my days; Let me know how transient I am. "Behold, You have made my days as handbreadths, and my lifetime as nothing in Your sight; surely every man at his best is a mere breath.

Psalm 39:4-5 (NASB)

There are several ways you can redeem the time and make the most of your few years on this earth. Each of the one hundred and one things listed below must be done with as much urgency as possible. You must work with the mind that the opportunity to do something will soon be taken away from you. When that day comes, you will wish you could come back and do any of the one hundred and one things on this "redeem the time" to-do list.

101 Ways to Redeem the Time

1. To redeem the time speaks of making the most of the opportunities God has given to you.
2. To redeem the time means to wait on the Lord as much as you can.
3. To redeem the time means to preach as often as you can.
4. To redeem the time means to pray as much as you can.
5. To redeem the time means to win as many battles as possible.
6. To redeem the time means to build as many churches as possible.
7. To redeem the time means to train as many Bible students as possible.
8. To redeem the time means to preach as many sermons as possible.
9. To redeem the time means to win as many souls as possible.

10. To redeem the time means to have as many conventions as you can.

11. To redeem the time means to hold as many Gospel campaigns as possible

12. To redeem the time means to baptise as many people as possible.

13. To redeem the time means to plant as many churches as possible.

14. To redeem the time means to preach the Gospel in as many countries as you can.

15. To redeem the time means to send as many missionaries as possible to as many places as possible.

16. To redeem the time means to ordain as many pastors as possible.

17. To redeem the time means to write as many books as possible.

18. To redeem the time means to preach on as many radio stations as possible.

19. To redeem the time means to preach on as many television stations as possible.

20. To redeem the time means to train as many shepherds as possible.

21. To redeem the time means to have as many shepherds' meetings as possible.

22. To redeem the time means to have as many church worker meetings as possible.

23. To redeem the time means to organise as many outreaches as you can.

24. To redeem the time means to organise as many breakfast meetings as possible.

25. To redeem the time means to organise as many school evangelistic programmes as possible.

26. To redeem the time means to distribute as many books as possible.

27. To redeem the time means to officiate as many weddings as possible.

28. To redeem the time means to do as much marriage counselling as possible.

29. To redeem the time means to have as many businessmen's fellowship meetings as possible.

30. To redeem the time means to have as many all-night prayer meetings as possible.

31. To redeem the time means to preach at as many dawn broadcast sessions as possible.

32. To redeem the time means to preach on as many buses as possible.

33. To redeem the time means to pass out as many tracts as possible.

34. To redeem the time means to anoint as many people as possible with oil.

35. To redeem the time means to pray for as many people to receive the baptism of the Holy Spirit as possible.

36. To redeem the time means to collect as much offering as possible for the Lord.

37. To redeem the time means to start as many building projects as possible.

38. To redeem the time means to dedicate as many church buildings as possible.

39. To redeem the time means to have as many prayer meetings as possible.

40. To redeem the time means to do as many twenty-one day fasts as possible.

41. To redeem the time means to do as many three-day fasts as possible.

42. To redeem the time means to have as many quiet times as possible.

43. To redeem the time means to work for as many hours for the Lord as possible.

44. To redeem the time means to organise as many crusades as possible.

45. To redeem the time means to give as much to the poor as you can.

46. To redeem the time means to give as many offerings as you can.

47. To redeem the time means to support as many crusades as possible.

48. To redeem the time means to sow as many seeds as possible in the lives of men of God.

49. To redeem the time means to help the poor and the handicapped as much as possible.

50. To redeem the time means to pray for the sick as much as possible.

51. To redeem the time means to oppose disloyalty in the church as much as possible.

52. To redeem the time means to do as many odd jobs in the church as possible.

53. To redeem the time means to encourage my pastor as much as possible.

54. To redeem the time means to visit as many sick people in the hospital as possible.

55. To redeem the time means to care for orphans as much as possible within the time I have.

56. To redeem the time means to sing as many songs in the choir as possible.

57. To redeem the time means to learn as many worship songs as possible.

58. To redeem the time means to spend as much time on my own with the Lord as possible.

59. To redeem the time means to be as holy as possible.

60. To redeem the time means to walk in love towards other people as much as I can.

61. To redeem the time is to overcome evil as much as I can.

62. To redeem the time is to not be offended as much as I can.

63. To redeem the time is to sacrifice as much as I can for the Lord.

64. To redeem the time means to try and lay hands on as many sick people as possible.

65. To redeem the time means to tell as many people as possible about Jesus Christ.

66. To redeem the time means to play as many leadership roles as I can in the church.

67. To redeem the time means to attend as many small group meetings as I can.

68. To redeem the time means to play as many instruments for the Lord as possible.

69. To redeem the time means to win back as many backsliders as possible.

70. To redeem the time means to help prevent as much of the stealing of God's money as possible.

71. To redeem the time means to protect church property as much as you can.

72. To redeem the time means to overcome as many temptations as possible.

73. To redeem the time means to overcome as many crises as possible in my life.

74. To redeem the time means to live as peacefully and happily with my spouse as possible.

75. To redeem the time means to train up my children as well as I can to serve the Lord.

76. To redeem the time means to give my whole family the greatest opportunity to serve God.

77. To redeem the time means to bring as many children to Sunday School as possible.

78. To redeem the time means to do as much secretarial service for the church as possible.

79. To redeem the time means to volunteer as much technical assistance to the church as possible.

80. To redeem the time means to volunteer as much of my computer skills to the church as possible.

81. To redeem the time means to volunteer as much of my architectural skills to the church as possible.

82. To redeem the time means to volunteer as much of my engineering skills to the church as possible.

83. To redeem the time means to volunteer as much of my legal skills to the church as possible.

84. To redeem the time means to do as much work for the church as possible without charging for it.

85. To redeem the time means to donate as much clothing to the needy as possible.

86. To redeem the time means to help the blind as much as possible.

87. To redeem the time means to feed as many hungry people as possible.

88. To redeem the time means to visit as many prisons as possible.

89. To redeem the time means to help as many prisoners as I can.

90. To redeem the time means to be as much like Christ as possible.

91. To redeem the time means to be as blameless as possible.

92. To redeem the time means to fulfil my ministry as much as possible.

93. To redeem the time means to be as obedient to the calling of God as possible.

94. To redeem the time means to fulfil my helps ministry as much as possible.

95. To redeem the time means to travel as much as I can in the name of the Lord.

96. To redeem the time means to help as much as I can with the translation of the Word of God into other languages as possible.

97. To redeem the time means to help with the interpretation of the Word as much as possible.

98. To redeem the time means to defend men of God as much as possible.

99. To redeem the time means to read as much of the Bible as I can before I die.

100. To redeem the time means to memorize as many verses in the Bible as possible.

101. To redeem the time means to attend as many camp meetings as possible.

Seven Reasons Why You Must Redeem the Time

1. *You must redeem the time because the days are evil.*

    See then that ye walk circumspectly, not as fools, but as wise, redeeming the time, because the days are evil. Wherefore be ye not unwise, but understanding what the will of the Lord is.

    Ephesians 5:15-17

Because the days are evil, you will find yourself engaging in evil activities as soon as you shift from activities that redeem the time. Indeed, we find ourselves in a hostile environment in which temperatures are below zero. You will quickly freeze to death in such an environment if you just sit down. Many years ago, our school was taken on a tour to the Tema harbour, one of the largest harbours in West Africa. Among the things we saw that day were these large cold stores, which were used to store fish brought in by trawlers. We went in and out of these huge cold warehouses because it was part of the tour.

I always remember thinking to myself, "What about if one of us was left in there by mistake. What would I do if I was mistakenly stuck in a huge freezer till the next day?" There is only one thing to do in such a situation: keep jumping, keep walking, keep moving until someone comes to open the giant freezer doors.

This is what has happened to Christians. We have been left in the huge freezer of this world and we must do everything to stay alive. Unfortunately, some people are settling down to relax in this dangerous freezing worldly environment. Surely, it must be understood that it is an evil day in an evil environment. The only thing to do is to redeem the time by rising up to do the only things that are wise to do in such a situation. Dear friend, be wise! Rise up, move around, get involved with the work of the Lord; otherwise you will perish with the world.

2. *You must redeem the time because it shows that you understand the will of God.*

> **See then that ye walk circumspectly, not as fools, but as wise, redeeming the time, because the days are evil. Wherefore be ye not unwise, but understanding what the will of the Lord is.**
>
> **Ephesians 5:15-17**

If you got locked in the large freezer I spoke about above, what would you do? What you do will show the depth of understanding that you have. Moving around would mean that you understand that your very life is at stake. Refusing to sit down at all would reveal that you understand that within moments you could lose your life. Jumping around, in spite of how tired you are, would reveal that you understand the desperation of your situation.

It is quite clear that most Christians do not really understand what is at stake. The lukewarm half-hearted approach to things of eternal value reveals that they have no sense of danger. It is clear that most Christians do not think that there is much at stake.

Desiring to be like the frozen fish in the freezer reveals the presence of an immature mind incapable of grasping the gravity of the situation. Indeed, Christians who spend their lives redeeming the time reveal that they are mature and truly understand why God wants us to be active, fruit-bearing, zealous and radical Christians.

3. *You must redeem the time because the night is coming when no one can work.*

I must work the works of him that sent me, while it is day: the night cometh, when no man can work.

John 9:4

"The night cometh, when no man can work" are the words of a man who knew that His life on earth was but a brief wisp of air, so transient in time that it was almost unrecognizable. The *night cometh,* but some act as though it will be day forever. Sometimes I play golf in the late afternoon and I am constantly aware that the night is coming. I can see the sun setting and I know I do not have much more time. I sense myself moving faster and picking up the pace because the night is coming. The night of your life may come in different ways.

Seven Ways in Which the Night May Come

a. Sometimes night comes in the form of pregnancy and childbirth in which a very active Christian woman may be relegated to the mothers' corner of spiritual inactivity for ten to fifteen years.

b. Sometimes, the night comes in the form of marriage to a person who opposes and prevents the Christian activities you have loved during the years before you got married.

c. Sometimes the night comes in the form of old age in which the energy and life needed for the work of God is simply not there.

d. Sometimes the night comes due to sickness which prevents you from doing what you would have loved to do. As I have grown older, I have found myself unable to fast in the way I used to fast when I was younger. At one point, I collapsed whilst waiting on the Lord all by myself. I really thought people would come and find my body on the floor. That is when I realised that I was not as strong as I used to be.

125

On another occasion, I recognized at least three different illnesses that were creeping on me due to persistent fasting, and I knew that the night had come when I would not be able to fast as much as I really wanted to.

e. Sometimes the night comes because you have graduated from a school that you have belonged to for many years. All the opportunities to win souls and to preach the Word of God in that school are gone forever.

f. Sometimes the night comes because you are forced to travel or migrate from a particular country or location. Many people have had to migrate because of war, economic situations or immigration issues. This has brought nightfall to many well-meaning Christians who wanted to continue working for God in a particular location.

g. Finally, nightfall comes because it is the end of your life on this earth. Death is the final and inevitable exit for all of us from the world of today. That night is coming to every man who is born to this earth. It is amazing how few of us even think of this reality that will happen to every man.

4. ***You must redeem the time because that is the only wise thing to do with your life.***

Unfortunately, many people do not treat time and opportunity as a special commodity. Time is something rare and precious, which God gives to all of us. It is the only thing you cannot regain or get back. When it is gone, it is gone forever. God's admonition to us is to use the time we have on earth to do as much for Him as possible. We must work while it is day. The only wise thing to do with your life is to redeem the time for the work of the Lord.

For all our days are passed away in thy wrath: we spend our years as a tale that is told. The days of our years are threescore years and ten; and if by reason of strength they be fourscore years, yet is their strength labour and sorrow; for it is soon cut off, and we fly away.

Who knoweth the power of thine anger? Even according to thy fear, so is thy wrath. So teach us to number our days, that we may apply our hearts unto wisdom.

Psalm 90:9-12

The poem below is the lamentation of a young man who had the call of God and the opportunity to serve the Lord. He put off this opportunity and acted as though he would live forever. The poem describes how the realities of life caught up with him and he exchanged a glorious life of soul winning for the fading treasures of this world. When he came to himself, it was too late to recover the time that he had lost.

Sunrise and skies are fair
A day begins without a care
A day for joy, a day for leisure
A day for thrills, a day for pleasure
Youth is merry and young, youth is gay
The great reaper is far away

But there is a call, 'tis the master's voice
I need you today, may I be your choice
A harvest is waiting and the fields are white
Will you join the reapers in the morning bright
Awake oh youth to the heavenly vision
Because Multitudes, Multitudes are in the valley of Decision.

The morning sun high above the earth
A cry of distress in the midst of mirth
Heathen are born and heathen are dying
Is there none to hear them crying?
"Oh yes," said the youth, count me as one
To help in this harvest till the day is done

Yet he lingered on for a little more fun
High sun, high noon
You'll be hearing from me soon.

127

I've married a wife, I've property to see
Five yoke of oxen acquired by me
I'll soon heed the call, I'll join the band
Ready to give the reapers a hand
But he carried on he had a bargain in hand

Afternoon sun and afternoon light
The golden ore hastened its flight
Conscience still hard memories daunted
Wealth; he had acquired, yet more was wanted
Many were the possessions he proudly flaunted
Houses and barns, lands and farms
Streams and ponds, stocks and bonds
Chickens and hogs, forest and logs
Crops and flack, meadows and haystacks
Orchards and berries, vineyards and cherries

Day was waxing, day was waning
Still the rich man was entertaining
For a sinister voice had spoken and said,
"On with the fun, on with the dance
Go ahead and make merry while you have the chance
You're a man of the times, you're ten feet tall"
He saw time yet for the call

So a little more jolly and a little more fun
And the hours slipped away until there were none
Sunrise to sun fall
The day was wasting on the western wall
Hands still busy with a thousand things
As evening descends and curfew brings
The day had faded into twilight red
As multitudes hasten to join the dead

"I am ready", "I am ready", said the man at last
But shaking hands could not hold fast

His hair unnoticed had turned to gray
Still he thought it was yesterday
Alas, harvest past, it was too late
To save those who had gone to a Christless grave

Where is the silver and where is the gold?
Where are the possessions to another soul?
Where are the sheep that grazed the hill?
And where are the cattle that drank from the river?
Where are the barns that were filled with plenty?
And where are the thoroughbreds one hundred and twenty?
Where are the heirlooms? Where are the treasures?
Where is the laughter? Where are the pleasures?
Where are the porters? Where is the wine?
Where are the delicacies? And the dinners that are so fine?

Sun sunk low. And night descended
The summer is gone, the harvest is ended
O for a chance for time extended!!
A wasted life was never intended!!
Sun fall and noon rise
What is left of the rich man's prize?
Go out to the valley to yonder hill
And see the marble standing still
Treasures were offered in heaven
But he took instead
The cold reward of the unsaved dead!

And what of us who live today?
This is our home let us not stay!!
A call to the harvest till it shall end
Work now, work fast, and reap my friend
New dawn and sun rise
Till the faithful the master will give the prize.

5. *You must redeem the time because your days will be few and full of trouble.*

My heart was hot within me, while I was musing the fire burned; then I spoke with my tongue: "LORD, make me to know my end and what is the extent of my days; Let me know how transient I am.

Behold, You have made my days as handbreadths, And my lifetime as nothing in Your sight; Surely every man at his best is a mere breath. Selah.

Surely every man walks about as a phantom; Surely they make an uproar for nothing; He amasses riches and does not know who will gather them.

Hear my prayer, O LORD, and give ear to my cry; Do not be silent at my tears; for I am a stranger with You, A sojourner like all my fathers. "Turn Your gaze away from me, that I may smile again before I depart and am no more.

Psalm 39:3-6, 12-13 (NASB)

Man that is born of a woman is of few days, and full of trouble.

Job 14:1

Even if you want to serve the Lord, you are living in a real world which is full of many diverse troubles. These troubles will serve as perfect distractions as long as you live. The troubles of this world will also serve as perfect deceptions to you. These deceptions have already captured the heart of millions. Because of the multitude of life's problems, few people ever think of eternity and the reality of Hell and Heaven even though it lies just a step away from us all.

Indeed, a clever trick has been played on the human race. Millions are sliding into eternity unaware of the great dangers just ahead. The rich and the poor alike will go to Hell because they do not know Jesus Christ. How surprised many poor people must be, when they discover that their problems will only intensify because they descend into Hell. Can you imagine the shock of the poverty/sickness-ridden masses who die only to descend into the abyss where there is even more weeping and gnashing of teeth?

But can you imagine the even greater shock that greets the millionaires, the big-shots, the politicians and the multitudes who live good lives on this earth, when they die and descend instantly into the darkness of the abyss?

Can you imagine their fright when they hear the sound of the wailing and screaming masses who are engulfed by the surging waves and gigantic sulphur flames of the lake of fire?

What a dangerous life it is to live at the edge of such an abyss, never even blinking an eye when a warning about eternal damnation is sounded! One millionaire said to me, "I'll take my chances. I believe there is no heaven and there is no Hell." Another rich man said, "There is nothing like hell and there is nothing like the devil. I will name my child Lucifer to prove to you that I do not believe that there is an iota of truth about Heaven, Hell or the devil."

It is amazing that the world makes a film and calls it *"Cliff Hanger!"* Indeed, it is so frightening to see people hanging off dangerous cliffs with their very lives in the balance. There is no need for any cliff hanging film! The whole world is hanging on a cliff anyway! Just look around you and you will see the souls falling off the cliffs of life everyday. You will see many others who could not care less that they are about to fall off the same cliff in the same way their friends just did.

6. *You must redeem the time because your life on earth is like a fixed contract.*

Is there not an appointed time to man upon earth? Are not his days also like the days of an hireling? As a servant earnestly desireth the shadow, and as an hireling looketh for the reward of his work: So am I made to possess months of vanity, and wearisome nights are appointed to me

Job 7:1-3

There is an appointed time for men on this earth. As I write this book, I am aware that my time is fixed. Sometimes I think to myself, "How long will I be here for? When will I go? How will I go out of this world?" These are questions I ask myself all the time. I think about eternity because I know the date for my entry into eternity is already fixed. Every day takes me closer to that date when my contract for this life will be over. Are you aware that your date of death has already been determined?

There are no new circumstances which are ganging up together to eliminate you from this world. Your date of death is fixed. We just have to rise up and work while we have the chance, redeeming the time and being wise. Every day takes us nearer to the end of our lease on this earth.

7. *You must redeem the time because your short life has an even shorter period of significance and fruitfulness.*

    He cometh forth like a flower, and is cut down: he fleeth also as a shadow, and continueth not.

    Job 14:2

    Whereas ye know not what shall be on the morrow. For what is your life? It is even a vapour, that appeareth for a little time, and then vanisheth away.

    James 4:14

    The grass withereth, the flower fadeth: because the spirit of the LORD bloweth upon it: SURELY THE PEOPLE IS GRASS. The grass withereth, the flower fadeth: but the word of our God shall stand for ever.

    Isaiah 40:7-8

Indeed, your life on this earth is short. But think about it; your short life will have an even shorter period of fruitfulness unto the Lord. You will only be able to do certain things for the Lord in *a particular season* of your life. The time before your season of fruitfulness will be non-scoring. Think about Jesus. He lived for thirty-three years but He only ministered for three out of those thirty-three years. He worked for God for three years out of thirty-three years which is only nine per cent of His entire life on earth.

In reality, we have a very, very short period of productive service for Jesus. Let us give our very best to the Lord!

CHAPTER 18

Forceful Evangelistic Christianity

I grew up in a Christian home and was made to attend church every Sunday. I must be honest, I found church very boring. I hated the long boring hymns and I couldn't understand the sermons. The priests looked unreal and detached.

I remember sitting through many boring and lifeless services at church. My main pre-occupation was to predict the time of the closure of the service. I would count the number of hymns on the board and estimate the closing time of the service.

You see, many priests and many church members are not born again. They are what you might call traditional Christians. One day, whilst at church, one of the priests who I think was an unbeliever announced from the pulpit how much beer the whole church had drunk the night before at a church function. The priest went on to say that one of the members owed him a carton of beer. He jokingly warned the member to deliver the carton of beer to his house. Indeed, there was nothing spiritual or meaningful about the service.

I can understand why many young people do not go to church anymore. It is just one meaningless, lifeless and boring ritual. If the pastor is not a born-again Christian, you cannot expect many members of the church to be born again.

When I first attended secondary school, at the age of twelve, I was an unbeliever. That is when I first came into contact with "real" born-again Christians. They were all members of the Scripture Union.

Though they seemed to be true believers, nothing about them attracted me. I remember one evening in particular, when the leader announced that there was going to be a Scripture Union meeting. I thought to myself, "Who would ever attend such a boring meeting?" These Christians were not attractive. They made weak and lifeless announcements inviting us, the unsaved, to join them. As a result, it did not occur to me to join this uninteresting group. I still cannot remember how I eventually joined the Scripture Union. I believe that the Spirit of God worked on me and drew me there without my even knowing it!

Many Christians are genuine and have a real message to give. But for a message to have any impact, it must be compelling. It must drive the listener to change! The message of the Lord Jesus Christ must persuade the unsaved to make a decision for Christ.

Then said he unto him, a certain man made a great supper, and bade many: And sent his servant at supper time to say to them that were bidden, Come; for all things are now ready.

And they all with one consent began to make excuse. The first said unto him, I have bought a piece of ground, and I must needs go and see it: I pray thee have me excused.

And another said, I have bought five yoke of oxen, and I go to prove them: I pray thee have me excused. And another said, I have married a wife, and therefore I cannot come.

So that servant came, and shewed his lord these things. Then the master of the house being angry said to his servant, Go out quickly into the streets and lanes of the city, and bring in hither the poor, and the maimed, and the halt, and the blind. And the servant said, Lord, it is done as thou hast commanded, and yet there is room.

And the lord said unto the servant, Go out into the highways and hedges, and compel [anagkazo] them to come in, that my house may be filled.

For I say unto you, that none of those men which were bidden shall taste of my supper.

Luke 14:16-24

This man had the unfortunate experience of spending a lot of money on a big party, inviting important people, only to find out that most of them were uninterested. This man was very surprised that his invitation was rejected. He became angry as he listened to the excuses of those he had invited. In his anger, he decided to invite anybody he found on the street. Imagine having a party with people you don't even know!

Unfortunately, at that time of the night, there were not so many people around. Even after inviting those on the street, his party was relatively unattended. He then decided to invite the sick, the blind and the handicapped. Imagine that! What an unusual selection of partygoers! His party was full of the non-entities of the community; the down-and-outs of society.

This story is symbolic of the Lord Jesus sending us out to invite people to Him. It is also symbolic of pastors sending out their members to evangelize the world. Every time I have embarked on evangelism, (inviting many people to a great supper) I have encountered the same things that this man encountered.

However, I believe this man had a successful party in spite of everything. The party came on and his house was full of guests. It might not have turned out the way he planned initially, but he had his party anyway.

You see, God is sending out evangelists to invite the whole world to know Christ. Unfortunately, many of those who are invited do not respond properly. The Jews were the first to be invited to know the Lord but they rejected Christ. This is how come the Gentiles also received their invitation.

Many of the elite who live in large urban centres, hear the Gospel over and over . However, they do not receive the Gospel. Instead, they criticize the preachers they see on television. Because of this, the Gospel is passed on to the poor people who will willingly receive the Word of God. In the passage above, the master asked his servants to compel people to come into the house. The word *compel* was translated from the Greek word *anagkazo* which means to necessitate, to drive, and to constrain by all means such as force, threats, persuasion and entreaties.

Why We Must Be Forceful

1. Driving persuasive Christianity is important because weak non-impactful evangelism will not work on this generation.

People are not going to be convinced or compelled to know God through our little church games. Our unexciting church anniversary programmes and bazaars will not force the world to pay attention.

2. Forcefulness is important because we must go to the highways and the byways with the Gospel.

If people are going to be touched with the Gospel, a new strategy of going to the gutters, highways and the bushes must be employed. Sitting in church and inviting people has long been an unworkable strategy for evangelism.

3. Without aggressive, compelling evangelism your church is going to be empty.

Remember that if this man had not employed the strategy of anagkazo he would have had an empty house. Remember also that, "A pastor without anagkazo will have an empty church."

4. **Without a compelling and constraining ministry your church will decrease naturally.**

The membership of a church is very fluid. Many people come but many people also leave. If you don't have more people coming in than those you are losing, your church will begin to decrease. If you don't want your church to close down, you must do what Jesus instructed – go out and compel people to come in.

5. **Life is becoming more hectic in the 21st century. Busy working people are going to have more and more excuses.**

The strategy of *anagkazo* will help you to overcome these excuses. Let me now take you through what I call the practical steps of *anagkazo*. These steps are derived from the story we just read in Luke 14.

Ten Steps to Persuasive and Compelling Evangelism

1. Prepare a great supper.

Anyone who wants to be used by God must prepare himself for the ministry. Today, God is using me in the ministry. This has not happened without thousands of hours of preparation. I realize that the sermons I preached to ten people some years ago are the same sermons I am preaching to thousands today. Preaching to a small group of ten people was part of God's preparation for me. So, if you want God to use you mightily, you must start preparing now! Take every opportunity you have to do something useful in the church.

Years ago, I remember playing the drums and the piano in my church. Though I didn't know it at the time, that was part of my preparation for ministry. Today, I know a lot about music and I can intelligently discuss anything that concerns music, worship or equipment. My experience with the music department has been a valuable asset to me.

2. *Do not keep to yourself but influence many people.*

You will notice that this man in Luke 14 held a great supper and invited many people. One of the primary reasons evangelism does not happen is because Christians keep to themselves. You cannot keep to yourself if you want to be an effective witness for the Lord Jesus Christ. When you sit on a bus, you can decide to be friendly to those nearby. Begin talking to the people around you. I always try to share the Gospel with people around me. I have always believed that I have some good news about Jesus. He has saved me and set me free.

During my second year in medical school, we lived on the beautiful Legon campus. We were transported daily to the other side of town where a teaching hospital was located. This involved a one-hour bus drive from one end of town to the other. I remember one day as I sat in the bus, I watched some senior colleagues take out condoms, blow them into balloons and fly them around the bus. As these students shouted and laughed over their lewd jokes, I realized how confident they were in what they were doing. We the Christians sat timidly in the bus like frightened sheep.

As I sat there, I decided not to keep to myself. I got the attention of everyone on the bus and began to preach. At that time preaching on the bus was unusual. Some of the students were angry with me and others were bored. Some looked out of the window in disapproval but I preached on! I decided not to keep to myself anymore. I decided to be like the man in Luke 14.

An *anagkazo* person does not keep to himself. I once lived in London where I felt stifled by the cold spiritual atmosphere there. I was used to preaching anywhere and everywhere. Everyone seemed so unfriendly and uninterested in Christianity.

One day, while sitting on the top level of a double-decker bus, the spirit of *anagkazo* rose up in me and I said to myself, "I cannot keep it to myself any longer."

I stood to my feet and to the surprise of everyone on the bus, I began to clap my hands to get their attention. I tell you, I may have looked bold on the outside, but I was scared on the inside. There were all sorts of murderous looking characters on the bus. But I maintained my cool and delivered a complete Gospel sermon.

The bus was quiet for a few minutes as they listened to this young mad man preach. I took my seat after preaching and got off at the next stop. One gentleman, who got off the bus with me, said to me, "I admire your courage! But I don't think you got very far." Whether I got very far or not is not what matters. What is important is that I preached the Word. And the Word always accomplishes something when it is preached.

> **…my word be that goeth forth out of my mouth…it shall accomplish that which I please…**
>
>

Isaiah 55:11

You see, any form of soul winning in our modern day and age, is going to have to be of the *anagkazo* type. Gentleness and meekness will not take you very far.

3. *Do not cancel your church programmes.*

Every pastor, in going through the normal processes of church growth, will experience highs and lows. But a pastor with the spirit of *anagkazo* will never cancel his church service. He will decide to press on no matter how many people attend.

One of my pastors told me how only one person attended church on a particular Sunday. He said that he had never felt so low. However, he managed to preach to that one soul and do his best for the Lord.

I remember when we had a very low attendance for one of our services. The Lord told me to do what this man in Luke 14 did: "Go out there and invite the community to church."

I said, "How can I do that on a Sunday?"

The Lord replied, "You do it, and you will be blessed."

I continued arguing with the Lord, "What will our Sunday morning visitors think? We will drive away people from the church."

However, the Lord insisted, "Go out and compel them to come in."

I obeyed the Lord.

I announced to the church that we were going to stop the service, go out into the community and invite them to come in.

I said, "We are going to go out to the community to bring them in."

I announced, "This is not a gentle invitation. Every single one of you must hold the hand of someone you see out there and physically bring them into the church building."

Some were taken aback. But we did it! And we brought in hundreds of "un-churched" people. That day we had several people giving their lives to Christ. We did this on numerous occasions and over a period, and that particular service increased in size dramatically. I was not prepared to close down my service because of low attendance. That is what any pastor with the spirit of *anagkazo* will do.

4. *Do not have an empty meeting.*

A pastor working with the spirit of *anagkazo* is not prepared to have any empty church service. Many years ago, whilst a medical student, the Lord asked me to start a church. I had no members in my church. Not even one soul to preach to! But I was not prepared to have an empty church.

I was still a student when the Holy Spirit directed me to the nursing students' hostel. I remember that very first day. It was around 5 a.m. and still dark. Standing outside the hostel, I clapped my hands and woke them up. They might have been surprised but that didn't bother me. I preached to them about Jesus. After I had finished I did something very bold. I said to them, "If you want to give your lives to Christ, change out of your night clothes, wear something decent and come downstairs. We want to talk to you about Christ outside."

That morning several young ladies gave their hearts to God. Twenty years later, some of them are still members of my church. Preaching at dawn to people in their beds has been one of my favourite methods of implementing this principle of *anagkazo*. One morning, I preached at the public health nurses hostel. A lady threw down a note saying she was a backslider and needed help. She wanted us to speak with her. That morning we ministered to her and God delivered her. She has been a faithful member of our church for the last twenty years.

Although I started out with an empty classroom, it soon became filled with nurses who had given their lives to Christ at my *anagkazo* dawn broadcasts. Dear reader, I want you to understand something. I did not inherit a church from anyone.

I have often gone to places where I knew no one, and no one knew me. I have had to go out and win souls, persuading people about the Lord, until the room was full.

5. *Do not be overcome by people's excuses.*

People are full of excuses for things they do not want to do. This *anagkazo* man in the Bible (Luke 14) listened to three amazing excuses for not attending his party. He was however not impressed by any of them.

The first excuse was about testing oxen in the night. Everyone knows that no one tests oxen at night. The second excuse was about somebody who had just gotten married. But we all know that a dinner would have been a nice outing for a newly wedded couple. The third excuse was about going to see some land in the night. Let me ask you a question. Would you not assess a piece of land before you buy it? How could you inspect a piece of land in the night? Would you even see it clearly? Yet somebody was using this as an excuse for not attending the party. Anyone who wants to reach people must not be deceived by people's excuses. He must learn to overcome people's excuses.

Even as you minister the Word of God, people form excuses in their minds. They develop reasons within themselves to disobey what you are preaching. Every good preacher must learn to preach *against* people's excuses and ideas. Jesus spoke directly *against* the people's reasoning and excuses. And they knew it!

...for they perceived that he had spoken this parable AGAINST THEM.

Luke 20:19

6. *Know that many excuses are empty.*

As I said earlier, many excuses cannot be substantiated. A good minister must learn to see through the emptiness of excuses. I spoke to one friend, inviting him to church. He in turn spoke about how the time was not convenient and how he had quite a distance to travel.

I said to him, "You are a successful businessman. Everything you want to do, you do. You travel. You get up early on weekdays. You even have time to visit your girlfriend who lives a few hundred kilometres away. How come you have no time for God?"

I told him, "If you really want to do something you can do it."

Some people do not pay their tithes because they claim they have no money. Watch how much money they spend on other things. You will realize that the problem is not a lack of money, but something more sinister.

7. *Know that many excuses are lies.*

There are many husbands who blame the inadequacies of their spiritual relationships on their wives and vice versa. I remember one fund-raising event in our church. During the fund-raising, the pastor asked for those who would like to give some money for the purchase of church instruments. A husband who happened to be a foreigner was prepared to give a donation. Just as his hand was going up, his wife pulled his hand down. She thought the pastor hadn't noticed.

After the service, the lady approached the pastor and said, "You know, the reason why we didn't give any money is because my foreign husband is so stingy." "I will see what we can do," she added. But that was an outright lie. It was actually her husband who wanted to donate something and she stopped him. People use excuses to cover their unwillingness to serve God. You must learn to go beyond every excuse that you hear.

8. *Make a way and do not give excuses.*

What differentiates the successful from the unsuccessful is the ability to overcome excuses. Notice that the man in Luke 14 was not moved by any of the excuses and reasons given. He made a way out of every excuse that was presented by the unwilling invitees.

If you really *want* to do something you make a way, if you *do not want* to do something you make an excuse! I recall when many young people were unwilling to come to church. The young men especially, made all sorts of excuses. The spirit of *anagkazo* rose up in me and I said, "If they will not come to church they will come to a party.

We organized a party for the young people in one area of the city. We made invitation cards and distributed them to the youth in the community. They were very happy and said to themselves, "This is another opportunity to 'jam'." I remember that evening in particular, we played upbeat Christian music and danced with the unbelievers. One of them told me later that he wondered why they were not being served with beer. At a point in the party, we switched to slower music and we said we had an announcement to make.

By that time, many of the hardened unbelievers were sitting around. To their surprise, I got up and preached the Gospel to them. They were surprised but still they gave their lives to Christ. Many were born again that night.

I have pastors in the church who were saved during some of these surprise evangelistic parties. You see, the Bible says by all means, "save some".

Anagkazo means to compel and to drive people to God. An *anagkazo* person is not moved by unfavourable circumstances. We were not moved by the fact that these young men did not want to attend a church. We made a way around that! Learn to make a way where there's no way. Find a way to overcome every excuse that people place before you.

9.   *Go out of your normal circle of life.*

Everyone has a circle of friends. The usual thing everyone does is to stay within his circle of friends and acquaintances. However, anyone who wants to be used by God must move out of his regular group. You will notice that the *anagkazo* man in this story was forced to move out of his normal circle of life. This is a reality that we must face if we want to please God!

When I was growing up in Accra, I had a group of friends. A sort of elitist company made up of children of foreigners and other bourgeoisie. As a child I travelled first class on intercontinental flights and interacted mainly with the so-called upper echelon of society. I stayed in international cities with my father. My hobbies were swimming and horse riding. You can imagine that in Ghana very few people had such pastimes.

However, there were hardly any Christians in these circles. When I got born again, I found myself moving out of this circle into a very different group. I moved out into better company, different from what I knew.

In order to please God I could not spend a lot of time in those circles anymore. There were simply no believers in that group. If you want to please God you will have to move out of your circle and get to know other groups of people.

I know that the rich man in this story would not normally fellowship with people who live in hedges or stand on highways. I know that the rich man in this story would not normally interact with cripples, the blind and the disabled. However, in order to achieve his goal, he had to interact with people of other social backgrounds.

In 1984, I was the leader of a nice fellowship at the university. We loved each other dearly and were good company for one another (actually, I found my wife in that group). Many of the people I knew in that little group are still my bosom friends up to this day. However, the Spirit of God impressed upon me to move out of our little group and to go to people we didn't know. I remember, some people were not in favour of expanding our nice little clique.

"If you bring in more people, we will lose something," they said. "There's something so special about this small fellowship. It's a cute little family."

But I led this group into one outreach after another, driving and necessitating people to come to the Lord. I was never tired of preaching. People are not tired of sinning, why should you be tired of spreading the Gospel?

During the second year of the medical school (which by the way is the most difficult year), I led this group in dawn broadcasts every Saturday morning. Everyone knew about us. They were used to our voices which rang out loud and clear every Saturday morning.

"Thank God for our nice little fellowship," I said. "But we have to go out there and win souls." We must move out of our little circle.

After awhile, unbelievers are no longer impressed with our sermons. If you do not rise up with a new approach, a new anagkazo method, your message will be ignored.

As we continued preaching at dawn, I realized that people just turned over in their beds and ignored us. I said to myself, "Our messages are no longer driving people to the Lord." But the Spirit of the Lord gave me a bright idea.

Since the people were now so used to our voices, we needed to do something new. I decided to send out a group to stand outside the doors of their rooms.

I told the preacher for the morning, "When you get to the altar call, we will start knocking on their doors."

I told him, "Tell the people who are listening to you they are going to hear a knock on their door. If they want to accept Christ they should open up and we will come in and lead them to the Lord."

The preacher followed my instructions. Suddenly, those who were ignoring us had to pay attention. We were knocking on their doors at 5 a.m.! Believe me, many were gloriously born again during those morning broadcasts. I vividly remember one brother in particular.

He would laugh at Christians as they spoke in tongues. He made fun of the gift of speaking in tongues. This is someone who would get drunk and lie by one of the many ponds that litter the beautiful campus of the University of Ghana. That morning as my friend the evangelist preached and said, "Perhaps you are hearing a knock on your door. If you want to be born again open your door and someone will come in and lead you to the Lord", I happened to knock on the door of this young man.

I was surprised when he opened the door and welcomed us in. He said, "I knew you would come to my room. Today is my day!" We prayed with him and he gave his heart to the Lord that very morning. To this day, this man is serving the Lord. I give glory to God for all the people that have been born again as we have forcefully moved out to speak the Word. *Anagkazo* works!

10. *Do not be satisfied as long as there is room.*

I love the song that says, *There's room at the cross for you.*

A pastor must never be satisfied as long as there is room in the church. The man in this story sent out his servants simply because there was room.

> **...and yet there is ROOM.**
>
> **Luke 14:22**

I believe that every church should arrange more chairs than people. The presence of empty pews should motivate the pastor to reach out until the house is full. The whole essence of evangelism is to have a full church.

> **...compel [anagkazo] them to come in, THAT MY HOUSE MAY BE FILLED.**
>
> **Luke 14:23**

Evangelism is not intended to be done in a vacuum. It should be related to church growth. All our efforts to lead people to the Lord should bear fruit. We must see our efforts filling church buildings. Whatever the case, a minister must see that there is room at the cross for one more soul. I believe that if we have this mind, God will use us to fill the church.

I have never been satisfied with the size of my church. When we had ten people, I wanted twenty. When we had fifty, I dreamed of a hundred. When God gave me one hundred people, I thought to myself, "What would it be like if I had five hundred people?" When the church was numbered in the hundreds, I thought, "What would it be like if we had thousands?"

We must be motivated to have a fuller house. These words keep ringing in my soul, "That my house may be filled!" "That my house may be filled!" Dear Christian friend, never forget that there is still room at the cross.

CHAPTER 19

John 3:16 – The Unchanging Purpose of Christianity

To me, this is the greatest verse in the Bible. It sums up the purpose for Jesus Christ's coming into the world. I see this Scripture as an anchor, which will help me stay near the heart of God's purpose for His church. I must be able to preach from this Scripture for several days, if need be. I want this Scripture to remain deeply embedded in my heart. I want to understand it with all its ramifications. I want to preach it. I don't want to just use it as a Scripture for witnessing. I want to tell every church that John 3:16 is still the most important Scripture for us.

> **FOR GOD SO LOVED THE WORLD, THAT HE GAVE HIS ONLY BEGOTTEN SON, THAT WHOSOEVER BELIEVETH IN HIM SHOULD NOT PERISH, BUT HAVE EVERLASTING LIFE.**
>
> **John 3:16**

1. *John 3:16 offers the greatest invitation of all time.* It is the great invitation that invites the whole wide world to come to God. It is the broadest invitation I have ever heard of. And it is the invitation from no other than

Almighty God. This theme of God inviting men to come to Him is repeated all through the Bible!

Ho, every one that thirsteth, come ye to the waters, and he that hath no money; come ye, buy, and eat; yea, come, buy wine and milk without money and without price.

Isaiah 55:1

Come unto me, all ye that labour and are heavy laden, and I will give you rest.

Matthew 11:28

And he said unto them, Go ye into all the world, and preach the gospel to every creature. He that believeth and is baptized shall be saved; but he that believeth not shall be damned.

Mark 16:15-16

2. *John 3:16 offers love from the greatest person ever to show love.* This offer of love comes from Almighty God Himself. Many people have mistakenly responded to the love of evil men only to experience pain instead of the joy they thought they would have. How could you reject the love that comes from your Maker, and the Creator of the universe? Women are so excited at the prospect of becoming the object of love and attention of an important person. So many women would like to marry presidents, millionaires, chiefs and even pastors. Dear friend, none of these can compare to the love of Almighty God Himself. All through the Bible, the scripture teaches about how great our God is. It is this great God who offers you His love.

Bless the LORD, O my soul. O LORD my God, thou art very great; thou art clothed with honour and majesty.

Psalm 104:1

Thy way, O God, is in the sanctuary: who is so great a
God as our God?

Psalm 77:13

For I know that the LORD is great, and that our Lord
is above all gods.

Psalm 135:5

For from the rising of the sun even unto the going
down of the same my name shall be great among the
Gentiles; and in every place incense shall be offered
unto my name, and a pure offering: for my name shall
be great among the heathen, saith the LORD of hosts.

Malachi 1:11

3. *John 3:16 offers the greatest kind of love.* There are
    different kinds of love. The love we speak of in John 3:16
    is the greatest love. It is the real thing. We are not speaking
    about a three-minute sexual experience. We are talking
    about a love relationship between a Father who is in Heaven
    and an undeserving miserable wretch like me. Wow! It's
    a big wow! This love is not something that diminishes or
    expires when the feelings go down. It is the love that is
    forever. All through the Bible,the Scripture teaches about
    how unique and how great God's love is.

For scarcely for a righteous man will one die: yet
peradventure for a good man some would even dare
to die. But God commendeth his love toward us, in
that, while we were yet sinners, Christ died for us.

Romans 5:7-8

Greater love hath no man than this, that a man lay
down his life for his friends.

John 15:13

Among whom we also all once lived in the lust of our
flesh, doing the desires of the flesh and of the mind,
and were by nature children of wrath, even as the

rest:-- but God, being rich in mercy, for his great love wherewith he loved us, even when we were dead through our trespasses, made us alive together with Christ (by grace have ye been saved;)

Ephesians 2:3-5 (ASV)

4. *John 3:16 offers love to the largest number of people ever possible.* Most people can love one or two people. Many women love only their husband and their two children. They have no time or space for anyone else. Their world comes crashing down when they realise that their husband's love is not as restricted as theirs. Many people do not have love for people who are not from their own country or tribe. Many people have no love for black people or white people because they are different. John 3:16 speaks about love, tolerance and kindness that is extended to all types, all colours, all shapes and all sizes of people. Even in the ministry, it is easy to notice how some pastors are simply prejudiced against other tribes or nationalities. Some churches cannot grow beyond their own tribes. And yet today, God is showing us that it is possible to love such a huge number of people. The Bible reveals how God has a great passion, attraction and desire to have all kinds of men come to Him.

The Lord is not slack concerning his promise, as some men count slackness; but is longsuffering to us-ward, not willing that any should perish, but that all should come to repentance.

2 Peter 3:9

I am debtor both to the Greeks, and to the Barbarians; both to the wise, and to the unwise. So, as much as in me is, I am ready to preach the gospel to you that are at Rome also.

Romans 1:14-15

5. ***John 3:16 offers the greatest gift ever offered to mankind.***
God's love and salvation cannot be compared to any amount
of money that a man can give to you. What shall it profit you
if you gained the whole world and lost your soul? The gift
of education, the gift of money, the gift of silver and gold,
cannot be compared to the gift of God's Son being given to
you. The free gift of God is eternal life through Jesus Christ
our Lord. I feel so happy as I share these thoughts with you.

**Jesus answered and said unto her, If thou knewest the
GIFT OF GOD, and who it is that saith to thee, Give
me to drink; thou wouldest have asked of him, and he
would have given thee living water.**

John 4:10

**For the wages of sin is death; but THE GIFT of God
is eternal life through Jesus Christ our Lord.**

Romans 6:23

6. ***John 3:16 teaches about the most important action a
human being can ever take – Having faith in Jesus Christ.***
The simple act of believing earns you the right to enter
Heaven. This simple reality makes the act of having faith the
greatest deed a human being could ever engage in because
nothing else can give you access to Heaven. Believing in
Christ is the greatest thing a human being can ever do for
himself. Becoming educated, acquiring money, getting
a visa, travelling abroad, buying a car, earning a PhD, are
not comparable to simply believing in Jesus Christ as the
Saviour. Jesus Christ Himself explains that simply believing
in Him is all the work you must do to get you into Heaven.

**Then said they unto him, what shall we do, that we
might work the works of God? Jesus answered and
said unto them, This is the work of God, THAT YE
BELIEVE on him whom he hath sent.**

John 6:28-29

7. *John 3:16 offers the greatest escape from prison known to man.* This great invitation in John 3:16, offers men the chance to make the greatest escape from the wildest prison ever created.

> **He that believeth on him is not condemned: but he that believeth not is condemned already, because he hath not believed in the name of the only begotten Son of God.**
>
> **John 3:18**

There is no prison like Hell. There is no torture and torment ever described that is comparable to what is spoken of Hell. And yet, we are offered the greatest unconditional release of prisoners ever known to man. There is no film which has an escape story as dramatic and captivating as this one. John 3:16 is the greatest "get out of jail free" card ever invented. Not going to Hell – not perishing is the essential reason why Jesus Christ died on the cross for us. HE WAS TRYING TO SAVE US FROM GOING TO HELL. Notice how the Scripture says, "that they might not perish."

How can we allow the world to go ahead and perish in Hell when John 3:16 is written for their benefit? How can pastors preach without telling people about John 3:16? It is the greatest betrayal to the world if we live without telling them about Hell and how to escape from it.

> **How shall we escape, if we neglect so great salvation; which at the first began to be spoken by the Lord, and was confirmed unto us by them that heard him;**
>
> **Hebrews 2:3**

> **And if thy hand offend thee, cut it off: it is better for thee to enter into life maimed, than having two hands to go into hell, into the fire that never shall be quenched: Where their worm dieth not, and the fire is not quenched.**
>
> **Mark 9:43-44**

8. *John 3:16 offers the greatest destination of Heaven and everlasting life.* Many people are excited when they have an opportunity to travel to a foreign country. There is excitement and joy because they are going to have a nice time. Dear friend, there has never been a more exciting destination offered to human beings than Heaven, the eternal home of Almighty God. Indeed, John 3:16 has once again offered the unthinkable and the unimaginable to mere humans like us. Is it possible that this invitation is to all of us? ⁷⁷The rich, the poor, the white, the black, the underprivileged, the forgotten and the famous? Wow! Indeed, this is a big wow!

For He looked for a city which had foundations, whose builder and maker is God.

Hebrews 11:10

Notwithstanding, in this rejoice not, that the spirits are subject unto you; but rather rejoice, because your names are written in heaven.

Luke 10:20

But lay up for yourselves treasures in heaven where neither moth nor rust doth corrupt, and where thieves do not break through nor steal:

Matthew 6:20